Suddenly the familiar voice of our
senior ground controller rasped in
my headphones, 'Red One Buster
Squadron, maintain your present
course and height. You should see
the bandit within a minute.
Our three aircraft seemed to wobble
simultaneously, as we all hunched
forward in our cockpits and peered
around. Almost immediately our
section leader bawled over the R/T
'Tallyho! Yippee! There he is, at
2 o'clock high.' I looked ahead and a
bit to the right, and there he was, a
Heinkel III, a few thousand feet
above and flying towards us. He saw
us almost simultaneously, and turned
diving steeply away as fast as he could.
I can't remember my thoughts as
I sighted my first Hun. I probably
felt a bit sorry for him; he obviously
hadn't got a hope against three
Spitfires . . .

Edited by David Guthrie

Spitfire Squadron

CORGI BOOKS
A DIVISION OF TRANSWORLD PUBLISHERS LTD

SPITFIRE SQUADRON

A CORGI BOOK 0 552 10326 8

First publication in Great Britain

PRINTING HISTORY
Corgi edition published 1976

Copyright © by David Guthrie 1976

Corgi Books are published by
Transworld Publishers Ltd,
Century House, 61–63 Uxbridge Road,
Ealing, London W5 5SA
Made and printed in Great Britain by
Cox & Wyman Ltd, London, Reading and Fakenham

FOR RUFUS

CONTENTS

EPIGRAPH

I see no lights of triumph
Only twisted hearts that turn no more
I see no singing regiments
Only the lads that
Pass and beckoning die.

A. A. Levy.

PREFACE

In September 1940 as a very young man, a Pilot Officer in a Spitfire squadron, I appreciated that Britain was at a climactic period in her history. My brother pilots and myself were very much at the sharp end because we were based in Kent – the Garden of England. But at that time it was no garden, for virtually every German raid flew through the skies over Kent after General Kesselring removed his force of Messerschmitt 109s from the Cherbourg Peninsula and placed all his fighters in the Pas de Calais region. The main force of German bombers was based farther inland behind the fighter bases, but they too had to pass over Kent to reach their targets. Five operational scrambles a day was by no means uncommon, and more often than not we would climb to 30,000 ft and beyond in an attempt to get at the top cover fighter screen comprised of Me 109s. Our Spitfires were, of course, unpressurized and we had to breathe pure oxygen. The affect of this on the human metabolism has still not been researched. The colon in the stomach would expand as the air became more and more rarified at altitude, and contract very suddenly as we dived at high speed. But we were all in the same boat.

In fact a fighter squadron can be likened to a monastery. There the great bells clang, and we lived a noisy life as the Merlin engines were started up with great regularity. Monks frequently indulge in prayer and so did we before take-off; there was no time for meditation when we were airborne. Monasteries are often situated in rural areas and fighter stations were too. Monks bury the dead brethren of their community and we invariably sent along an officer to attend the burial service of one of our colleagues who had been killed, those posted missing went to unknown graves. However, monks are normally intact when they die and here we differed from them. A Spitfire which dives into the ground at 500 mph with the pilot still aboard can dig its grave as much as thirty feet deep. Small hope that his body would be intact, so the diggers had no alternative than to put his remains into a jam-pot or a biscuit tin, depending on what they found. His relatives would not know this, of course, nor was it our duty to explain such circumstances. But they would have become suspicious if a very light coffin were solemnly carried by six bearers and deception would have been impossible. So we used to fill the coffins with sand-bags to make up the weight of a man, even though there was only a jam-pot in it, in order to conceal the true facts.

However, I invited several of my colleagues to write about their experiences and some of them, of course, were killed in action before they managed to finish their narratives. They were by no means eager to take up my invitation, but by dint of persuasion I somehow gained sufficient material to make a book out of it all, although this was not achieved until about the Spring of 1941. By that time the Luftwaffe had abandoned their daylight raids on London, except for high-flying fighter/bombers which dropped their bombs at random. In some respects these presented even more difficulties to us than the massive daylight attacks in the summer of 1940, because the Messerschmitts were flown in at top speed and great height, and our radars were by no means as effective as they became later. Our basic method of interception at this time was to fly standing patrols at squadron strength over the general area of Kent and Sussex. Generally speaking, this represented sound tactics and a great number of bombs were jettisoned long before the German pilots got as far as London. But the moment this happened, the Messerschmitts became fighters in their own right, not fighter/bombers, and we had to tread carefully.

With this background, the evidence I lay before the reader was written by several young men – I once calculated the average age of the pilots in the squadron and the answer was twenty-one years old. They were not authors, of course; nevertheless, some of them wrote brilliantly. They came from all sorts of backgrounds, but what they had in common was a basic education good enough to enable them to learn to fly the Spitfire – which demanded fairly high scholastic standards. However, after they had completed their stories, they all met sudden death in the course of time, either in action or through flying accidents. I personally witnessed the final act of some of them; in other cases I did some detective work and discovered the manner in which they came to grief. It was all very sad.

But to turn these personal accounts into book form demanded obituary notices, for readers would be dissatisfied if they were not given some description of the men, written by one who stood and watched. So I did exactly that. Another task I set myself was to edit their stories, for the jargon we used in 1940 would be incomprehensible to modern readers, apart, that is to say, from those of Churchill's 'Few' who are still breathing. But in the editorial process I did my best to allow their narratives to stand, to leave their style of writing almost exactly as it was when they scribbled away while waiting for yet another order to scramble. Even so, there is bound to be some repetition in these personal accounts, because we shared almost identical experiences. But as they all used their own descriptive powers and as each chapter is obviously written by a different hand, I thought that would be appropriate enough.

Readers might find this to be a most exciting book. But for my part, Shakespeare summed it up very well: 'It is a melancholy of mine own, compounded of many simples, extracted from many objects, and indeed the sundry contemplation of my travels, in which my rumination wraps me in a most humorous sadness.'

EDITOR'S NOTE

For obvious reasons I have disguised the identity of the particular Spitfire squadron referred to in this book. I have also given pseudonyms to the pilots who wrote their narratives in 1940–41. Had I not done so, the relatives who survive my erstwhile colleagues might have got to know about the manner in which they were killed. It was no part of my job as editor to resurrect such painful memories: I found my task painful enough in any case.

CHAPTER ONE

JOE

SMITH was my engine fitter and old enough to be my father. I was nineteen and he was over forty, yet he had to call me Sir which was a bit bloody silly. It wasn't so bad for my airframe mechanic because he was only about twenty-five. On the other hand, I had to do the hard-arsed work in the air, although the ground crews got bombed now and again on the ground. I joined Buster Squadron in January 1940 and it hadn't long been equipped with Spitfires, after using Gauntlets. So by August when the heat came on, I was senior enough to have my own Spitfire together with Smith and Brown, except when it went into the hangar for an inspection. Rather like Don Quixote and his squire I suppose. Of course my Spitfire was not the same one all the time because I kept getting shot down. On the other hand, I reckon I was shooting down more of those German bastards than they were hitting me up the backside. I hardly bothered to make any claims for the Germans I shot down; anyway the Intelligence Officer wouldn't have believed me, the sour-faced old holier-than-you sod. It was to him merely an exercise in statistics; he never got a bullet up his bum in his life, and he never will so long as the war lasts, if you ask me.

Buster Squadron moved from 12 Group to the hot seat in 11 Group towards the end of August. Then we were really in the shit. It's all very well having a bang at a lone reconnaissance Hun in 12 Group when you've got another couple of chaps on your wing. But it's not quite the same in 11 Group when you run into three hundred bloody bombers escorted by another three hundred Me 109s and there are only twelve of us. They are all looking out for you, which means there are a couple of thousand German eyes scanning the skies and all we've got are twenty-four eyes. In any case,

I am a bit short-sighted and only scraped in as a pilot for that reason. I'm not like Butch, who is long-sighted. He could see a flea on Hadrian's Wall from two miles away. That's why we use him as one of the weavers. I couldn't be a weaver, criss-crossing above the squadron and acting as look-out. They would have me in the back quicker than you could say knife and the boys below would also cop it.

My God, I remember the first time I was shot down; it was on August 30th. I had got this Me 109 nicely lined up in the gun-sight at an angle of about 15 degrees. I had given the Spitfire full boost and she was still accelerating, so I must have been doing about 350 mph. I'd got him cold but was about 400 yards out of range, so I had to wait a few seconds to make up the distance. But his friend von bloody Hindenburg was diving at me all unbeknown, and I couldn't take my eyes off Fritz when it was all so near but yet so far. There was a hell of a bang and the Spitfire flicked into a spin; just as well or Hindenburg would have finished me off, I guess. But I had a deuce of a job getting out of it and wrestled with the Spitfire like a chap confined in the dangerous ward at Colney Hatch. However, I managed to get out of the spin and had a look out of the window. Then I saw the reason why. The bastard had just about shot off my port aileron. When I arrived in a safe area – if there was a safe area anywhere in the skies of Kent – I quickly gave her a stalling test. She tried to flick into another spin at 100 mph, but I managed to evade it. Had I not, it would have been curtains because I was then at only 5,000 ft, and I lost 15,000 ft getting out of the previous spin. So I decided I could not possibly land with the undercarriage down, else I would be going so fast when I hit the deck that I would overshoot into the barbed wire at some speed.

My R/T wasn't working so it was impossible for me to inform the Duty Pilot on the ground of my predicament. I throttled back when I arrived over the airfield and watched a squadron of Hurricanes take off before attempting to land. My flaps weren't working, which made the whole thing that much more hazardous, but I managed to get the Spitfire lined up for landing. I was darned if I would attempt to belly-land her on the runway, for she might have caught fire when the sparks flew; so I decided to put her down on her belly parallel with the runway on the grass. This brought about another problem. They had filled in the bomb craters of the runway and shoved some tar over them; but there were craters in the grass alongside. So I had no alternative but to bring her down to just over 100 mph on the approach, put the airscrew into fine pitch so it would not make the same impact as if in coarse pitch when we hit the deck, and when I was at 50 ft I said a prayer – Christ help me.

She shuddered as we hit the grass and the engine came to a sudden halt when one blade of the prop got itself buried in the ground. A hell of a lot of dust rose as we continued on our way, but she came to a dead halt in about fifty yards. I had tightened my straps and wasn't thrown forward by the quick deceleration, although the straps nearly broke on impact. Then I shoved the cockpit canopy back – why hadn't I thought of that before? – and started to unstrap myself in case she caught fire. At one moment I thought she was on fire because clouds of dust descended which looked exactly like smoke. But I had kept my oxygen mask on to save my face from being slashed wide open and I gave myself a boost of emergency oxygen to keep the dust away and also to give me a little bit more heart. I had lifted my goggles from my eyes in case they smashed on impact, so I could hardly see for dust. But I felt my way out of the cockpit and scrambled down on to the wing.

By this time the fire-engine had arrived and the blood-wagon was not far behind, and the firemen gave me a hand as I staggered on to the grass. They removed me a safe distance away from my Spitfire in case she blew up, but I told the Sergeant in charge to stop mucking around with me and keep a good eye on the Spitfire because I didn't want her to blow up. She was obviously Category Three meaning that she was repairable or could be used for spare parts, but if she caught fire she would be Cat. Four – a write-off. And we were getting desperately short of Spitfires. The Sergeant had a small bottle of rum in his pocket and gave it to me. It did me a power of good.

Captain Albert Ball was my hero when I was a schoolboy. He finished up with a VC, DSO and MC in the Royal Flying Corps. His favourite aeroplane was the Nieuport Scout; mine is the Spitfire, but I don't expect I will have anything like his success in this war. What worried me when

I applied for a commission in the RAF was firstly whether I would pass the eyesight test – my educational qualifications were pretty good funnily enough – and then whether I would be sent to Fighter Command after I had qualified as a pilot. I didn't want to be sent to a flying-boat squadron or anything like that, certainly not bombers. I had no desire to drop bombs on the Germans, but I quite liked the idea of shooting the bastards down in the air. Nor would I have much enjoyed being posted to a Hurricane squadron; there is no comparison between the Spitfire and the Hurricane. The former is a race-horse and the Hurricane is an old cab-horse so to speak. So I was lucky to get what I wanted, very lucky in fact. Being slightly short-sighted is, of course, a handicap, because in fighter combat the essential requirement is to see the Hun before he sees you. And the sky is a mighty area, anybody's vision fades slightly at great height when breathing pure oxygen, and you also get spots before your eyes in any case. However, it is possible to train your eyes to focus almost beyond infinity by dint of exercising the optics, which I do. I just look into the sky and strive to see the stars in a manner of speaking. When you're flying on instruments, your range of vision is short, but when you then scan deep into the skies, you have to change from near-sightedness to very long distance immediately. It's all very difficult.

Another thing I had to do was to forget about flying an aircraft just for the sake of it. A Spitfire isn't an aeroplane, it's a flying gun-battery. Of course you have to be able to take-off and land, to get out of spins, to fly on instruments in cloud and so forth. But it is really a flying machine-gun – or rather eight machine-guns. You don't bother about keeping the skid and slip indicator steady and all that when in combat; in fact this would make it easier for the Hun to shoot you up the backside. But if you are shoving your boots coarsely on the rudder-bars, then the aircraft is skidding like hell, and if Fritz took a pot-shot more likely than not you would skid out of harm's way. In any case there is not a moment available to gaze at the instrument panel in combat; your eyes are either craning round with your neck or peering into the mirror which shows what is coming up behind, or fixed on the gun-sight as you make ready to press the firing button. It's all rather like women really. They all look the same in bed when the light is out. They aren't worth anything much but they can accommodate a man in bed. That might sound a bit stupid, but somebody ought to work it out.

So a Spitfire, although a beautiful piece of machinery, is really a flying gun-battery, which brings up the point of aerial marksmanship. I'm damned if anyone taught me how to shoot straight during my flying training courses, but I can shoot straight. That's another silly use of words because you don't shoot straight when you are aiming at a member of the Luftwaffe – you shoot crooked. I know that I can shoot crooked because I've downed about six Huns already – more likely downed ten; but that sour-faced old sod would only allow me six claims. He did also give me four probables or damaged, but then he doesn't know the arse end of a Heinkel from its front, except on paper. I doubt if he's ever seen a Dornier considering he crawls into an air raid shelter the moment the sirens go. I once landed with my windshield covered in oil from a Heinkel that blew up when I hit it with my de Wilde ammunition. He almost suggested that he should take the oil to a laboratory to make sure it had been made in Germany; that's the sort of silly old sod he is. He says he's a senior Wrangler, but as far as I am concerned he can go take a jump off the Eiffel Tower – top story.

The way I learned to shoot crooked in a Spitfire came about because I had to shoot crooked to knock down the odd partridge about my father's house. It's strange but fixed gun marksmanship is almost identical to making the best use with a shot-gun at birds on the wing. If a pigeon is flying at 400 ft and you shoot at it you are wasting your cartridges, you haven't got a hope in hell because it is out of range. It's the same with Messerschmitts. The Browning batteries of machine-guns are only effective at around 400 yards range; if you use them at 500 yards you might be lucky but you probably won't be. There is a thing called bullet drop for a start, meaning that a bullet dropped from your hand would fall to earth immediately. But if it tears out from your guns at 2,000 mph it is still dropping through gravity even if only imperceptibly. After about 300 yards, as the muzzle velocity diminishes, it begins its descent with great vigour. So obviously one has to be in range of the Hun before pressing the tit. And of course the closer you are to your target the less likely you are to miss. If a man put a pistol in your back and pulled the trigger he could not fail to miss, to make the point. However, one cannot get too close to a German aircraft because the forces of slip-stream from its propellor would make it impossible to hold the Spitfire; she might even be turned over on her back. Equally, whereas it is a good thing to be skidding like hell when a Jerry is coming up behind, when you yourself are aiming, the Spitfire must be absolutely steady – your own skidding would make the bullets miss.

Range estimation is the most important aspect of fixed gun marksmanship and it covers up for the other errors if you are at the closest practical range. But, of course, to close the range adequately is a stroke of luck. More often than not you have to take a pot-shot and hope that you have got the various equations right. Assuming you are in range, and depending on the angle the enemy aircraft represents, the next most important thing is deflection or lead, or angle off. If you aim at a Me 109 flying at 300 mph on a beam attack then you have to aim well ahead of it else your bullets would pass well behind him due to the time interval. If you were lucky enough to sneak up behind him on a dead astern attack, you wouldn't have to use any deflection whatsoever. But in between those two extremes is how you normally have to aim, and it is all very complicated. Then there is his angle of flight to take into consideration. If he is diving, you must aim below his flight path because of the time it takes for bullets to arrive at the target; similarly, aim above if he is climbing. But as I said, the closer one is to the target the less the effect of other possible errors. The whole business is analogous to shooting pheasants on the wing, and that is where I learned these arts, not from RAF training.

There was one particular German who knew the arts of fixed gun firing far too well for my liking. The funny thing about fighting the Luftwaffe is that one is concerned with the enemy aircraft not the man or men inside it; they just have to take their chance. I never knew how many men were killed when shooting down a bomber and, frankly, I never cared too much about that. They were under orders to penetrate British air space and they had no right to be there. So it was my duty, and I was also under orders, to kill them if I could. But this particular Hun could shoot crooked enough to get me. There was a whirling dog-fight one day and I neglected to look into my rear-view mirror because I was concentrating on a Me 109. In any case it was almost impossible to differentiate between a Spitfire or Hurricane or Messerschmitt at such a moment. The sky was alive with fighters and I distinctly remember three parachutes with men attached to them floating down slowly to earth. Anyway, before I could thumb my firing button I was hit by a 20 mm cannon shell. It struck the Merlin engine in the Spitfire and I saw flames beginning to lick from the exhaust tubes towards the cockpit.

This presented two problems. First I had to remove the German from my tail. Next I had to get the hell out of my Spitfire. I pulled the throttle right back, switched off the two magnetoes, and hauled back on the stick in a tight turn, tightening it until I hit the threshold of blacking out. The Spitfire was more manoeuverable than the Messerschmitt, and in any case, with a dead engine the turn would be much tighter than if one were flying at speed. After pulling round in three turns, the sky behind me seemed to be empty of any aircraft but flames were spreading and the cockpit was beginning to feel hot. Now there was no time to lose, so I heaved open the cockpit canopy which, fortunately, was not too iced up for the purpose, undid my safety harness, took a deep breath of oxygen and then removed my flying helmet plus the oxygen mask. I levelled the Spitfire out, clambered on to the seat, and pushed the stick forward with my boot. This applied negative gee which hurled me out of my cockpit and I rose above the Spitfire like an angel returning to Heaven. And because I hit the control column with my boot she went into a dive. I spun like a top, in thin air, fumbled for the rip-cord of the parachute with my gauntleted right hand, found it and then decided to wait. I was still moving through the air at about 200 mph, and my back might have been broken if the parachute made me come to a sudden halt. On the other hand it might not open at all. Furthermore, I might fall into a state of unconsciousness through anoxia due to lack of oxygen. I had left my Spitfire at 25,000 ft and the air was very rarified. But when I felt the sense of exhilaration which portends the arrival of a state of anoxia, I gave the ripcord a hefty pull whilst at the same time indulging myself in prayer. There was a back-breaking jerk as the great canopy of the parachute flew open above me. Then I was seemingly stationary, high in the sky half-way between heaven and hell.

Before I lost consciousness through anoxia, I dimly saw my Spitfire explode 10,000 ft below into a million pieces of duralumin. At about 15,000 ft as I estimated it, I slowly recovered my senses and saw below me a heavily wooded area which contained mighty English oak trees which some-one had planted three hundred years ago. The wind was drifting me towards this area. I hit a tree with a thunderous sound as my boots and then my body smashed into the foliage. And I covered my eyes with my gauntleted hands to avoid having my eyes gouged out. Then I unlocked my parachute harness, and dropped on to a trunk of the tree which had a sweet smell to it. I paused for breath and scrambled down, hanging on to the tree as I did so. I dropped to the ground and found myself surrounded by members of the Home Guard who took me to be a German and were prepared to rough me up. My vocabulary in terms of invec-tive and abuse is fairly comprehensive, and these old men were rather shocked when I explained to them that they were a bunch of four letter words. However, they did insist that I should be taken to the nearest interrogation centre which was in Maidstone. After this little farce, a RAF car was called from the nearest airfield and I was driven back to rejoin Buster Squadron.

The Air Transport Auxiliary was comprised of civilian pilots, some of whom were women. I don't want to be disparaging but some of them couldn't ride a bicycle let alone fly a Spitfire. I do admit they did a good job in that they ferried fighters from the manufacturers' airfields to the squadrons, but their accident rate was terrible even though they, so to speak, released operational pilots from this chore. I had telephoned my squadron from Maidstone using Army lines and told them to get me a new Spitfire double quick sharp. The organization was superb (apart from the ferry pilot scheme) and the next morning I saw my aircraft join circuit, land and then topple on to its nose. This bent the blades of the propeller and meant that the engine would have to be shock-tested. The ATA pilot had landed too fast, using his brakes like he was in control of an elephant not a Spitfire, and thereby bent my aircraft to such an extent that it would never be repaired within a fortnight. I didn't speak to him when the blood-wagon arrived and deposited him at the squadron hut; but I felt like strangling him. I borrowed another Spitfire that day and on the following morning another one arrived which fortunately the ATA pilot didn't prang. They soon painted my personal letters on the fuselage, then with the aid of the squadron armourers I harmonized the guns.

The Spitfire has two batteries of four machine guns set on either side of the propeller outside the arc as it rotates. They are quite widely dispersed, whereas those in the Hurricane are close together because of the thicker wing-root. This makes the Hurricane a better gun-platform because the fire is more concentrated, but the Spitfire is streets ahead in every other respect. The Hurrie pilots do quite well with their old hacks mainly because there are a lot more Hurricanes in Fighter Command than Spitfires. Consequently, there is a greater proportion of experienced fighter pilots flying Hurricanes than in our case. To harmonize the guns, the aircraft has to be jacked up by the tail until it is in a straight and level flying attitude, which is done at the gun butts. Then periscopes are inserted in one gun barrel at a time so you can see exactly where the gun is pointing vis a vis a target. This is repeated for every gun which is then adjusted until a cone of fire is established at the preferred range. I could have chosen a range of 350 yards where the bulk of the bullets would converge, but I always harmonized at 250 yards. The 0.303in bullet represents very light armament compared with the 20 mm cannon of the Me 109, even though the rate of fire per gun is 1,350 rounds per minute. Anything over 250 yards might strike a German aircraft, but it probably wouldn't do lethal damage. In any case, all we have is de Wilde ammunition which is supposed to be incendiary and would burn on impact but the Luftwaffe have got high-explosive heads to their cannon shells, together with armour piercing, incendiary and God knows what.

While I was harmonizing the guns with the armourers, other ground crews were sticking transfers of my squadron letters on the sides of the fuselage; the RAF roundels had, of course, been painted on at the factory. When all was ready I had to give her an air test because she was strictly a non-operational fighter until I declared her fit for operations. As I was taxiing out I saw a red Verey cartridge explode high in the sky from the Duty Pilot's hut. Then the chaps came running out to their Spitfires. It was a scramble order all right. I put the brakes on and came to a stop a discreet distance away from the taxiing area of the squadron and watched the white smoke emanating from the exhaust stubs of twelve Spitfires as the ground crews started up the engines ahead of the pilots' arrival. There was a great flurry of dust as the aircraft moved out of line and the pilots taxied as fast as was prudent without pranging their Spitfires. Ours was a grass airfield at this stage of the game and we could taxy in echelon formation, six in each echelon, meaning we were fast reactors to the scramble order. When we moved later to Biggin Hill where there was a concrete runway, our reaction time slowed quite considerably.

The squadron roared into the air and I followed shortly afterwards. I put the R/T on the interception frequency and listened in as the controller gave directions to my squadron commander. But I flew on a northerly heading to get into a safe area while I gave the Spitfire an air test. She flew one wing low when I reached 200 mph and it needed all my strength to stop her rolling on to her back when I hit 350 mph. Apart from that she was fine in all attitudes. When I arrived at 25,000 ft I decided to put her into a spin to see whether she came out or whether I went out on the end of my parachute. I shut the throttle, climbed her until she began to judder as she stalled, kicked the port rudder bar, her nose dropped vertically and she began to spin like hell. Hazy crazy it was as the earth turned round at such high speed. I gave her hard right rudder and put the nose even farther down, then the rate of rotation gradually began to decrease. When she was in a straight dive I eased back on the stick, pulled harder and regained some of the height I had lost. When I landed, I would have to tell my airframe mechanic to adjust for left wing low, and the accuracy of his work would rely entirely on my exact interpretation as to the extent of the fault. If he didn't get it right first time, I would have to put myself non-operational until such time as we worked out the snag together.

I headed south and saw Canterbury Cathedral slide under my wing-tip. Then the controller rang up Buster Squadron and told my commanding officer that the main German formations were already back over the Channel and there was no hope of intercepting them. I cursed and wheeled over to get on a nor-westerly course for base. Then the controller rang up again to say that a lone bandit was heading south from the area of Chatham. Crispin, my squadron commander, ordered a section to detach and go after it. He gave his position as over East Grinstead, which meant I was in a much better position to make a swift interception than Yellow Section which had been detached. The controller then said he had ordered the anti-aircraft artillery to open fire on the bandit, not that they had any hope of hitting the German aircraft because their aiming was awful and their fuses failed on more occasions than not. But I dimly saw ack-ack shells explode in the area above the Medway. I broke the seals on my throttle quadrant which gave me emergency boost, and the Spitfire shuddered under the strain. I followed the puffs of ack-ack fire until I saw a dot in front of my eyes. I closed on it very fast, although I was almost breaking my right wrist to keep the Spitfire in a straight and level position against its left wing low tendency, and I then recognized it as a Heinkel III.

But how to attack it. My right hand was tugging at the control column, holding up the port wing as well as I could. But I needed the right thumb to press the firing button because the left hand was essential to moving the throttle. I estimated that the Heinkel was flying at about 170 mph and it was obvious that I would have to come into the attack as slowly as possible because my port aileron was mal-adjusted. But if I closed in a dead astern attack at merely 200 mph, then I would be a sitting duck for the German gunners in the bomber. Thus there was only one thing to do, which was to make a head-on attack. If I did so at 200 mph the closing speed of my aircraft and his would be about 400 mph, but I could hold my left wing straight and level well enough to sight accurately. A head-on attack is, of course, a case of gross optimism – certainly in fighter to fighter combat, when the closing speed might be 700 mph which would give one only a few seconds to aim at a fleeting target. But in this case, as the Hun was flying comparatively slowly probably because his bomber had been damaged during another interlude, it could come off. Anyway, I could think of no other option under the circumstances.

Accordingly I flew past the Heinkel about a mile and a half on his starboard side, and kept him in view by craning my neck until I was a couple of miles ahead of him. Then I went into a steep turn to port, which helped my wrist which was by now painful from having held the port wing up at high speed, and pulled into a tight turn when I reckoned I had sufficient distance between him and me to get my gunsight aligned. I centred on him as he approached, or I approached, and lined him up with the bead of my gunsight. He started to weave when he realized I was in a head-on position, but I could follow those manoeuvres without too much difficulty. By this time I had reduced speed to about 200 mph and could handle the Spitfire well enough. I pressed the tit at about 600 yards because he would be flying into my bullets, although in theory he was out of my range. I kept my thumb stabbed on the firing button and watched the tracer mixed up with the de Wilde hitting the twin engine bomber. When I closed to 150 yards it was time to get the hell out and I hauled back on the stick to pull her up and out of harm's way. But I had misjudged it.

The Heinkel exploded and bits of flying debris hit my Spitfire as I crossed above it. I continued in a great climb but I felt pieces of metal striking my Spitfire. Then my oil tank burst and washes of the oil made in Germany flew past me, but some of it stuck on my windshield, meaning I could see nothing. I looked down at the instrument panel and saw the glycol gauge indicating hot as hell, and the oil pressure had dropped to nil. There was nothing left but to switch off the engine and the propellor sighed to a halt. Then I tore the cockpit canopy open and stuck my head out so I could see. Below me was West Malling airfield and although I took note of the bomb craters there was still plenty of room in which to make a belly landing which I eventually achieved.

Goddamit, here was a brand new Spitfire which again had to go back to the factory for repair or salvage. On the other hand I must have killed at least four members of the Luftwaffe when the Heinkel blew up. And that's the name of the game.

*   *   *

Joe was mechanically minded. He went to Oxford to study physics, but left after Munich because he saw that

*war was imminent and joined the RAF. He was lucky to
attain his desire to be posted to a fighter squadron because
the system of selecting pilots under training was lunatic. In
due course, after the war broke out, the selection process
was handed over to psychiatrists some of them female and it
then became positively maniacal. I could tell a born fighter
pilot just by looking at him for five seconds, which also means
that I could diagnose when a pilot posted to Buster Squadron
was totally unsuited to the role of fighter pilot. But if they
had sent Joe to fly bombers or flying boats he would have
gone mad. There were some excellent potential bomber
pilots in Buster Squadron and they were the first to be killed
in action because their reflexes were simply not sharp
enough. As a fighter pilot Joe nearly rated as a genius, but
his eye-sight was not sharp enough for him to be placed in
that bracket. As he says, you've got to see the Hun before he
sees you, that is the be-all and end-all. If you don't, then
you get a dose of hot lead up your backside. If you do,
certainly in Joe's case, Fritz gets a shocking pain in his
backbone just before he goes to meet his Maker, for Joe was
a brilliant fixed gun marksman. He studied the subject
keenly, even though he knew the principles very well
from his experience in attending organized game shoots —
especially partridges which usually present flying targets.
But Joe, despite his tender years, killed a record number of
woodcock in one shoot, or so I remember him telling me,
and they present possibly the most difficult of targets.*

*Joe was burly in build and stocky. His hair was auburn,
his eyes blue and he was a crack squash player — indicative
of his sharp reflexes. He was related vaguely to an earl but
he was no snob. He was probably Buster Squadron's most
respected officer among the ground crews, because although
he was not familiar, he certainly pulled their legs no end.
He was also one of our youngest pilots, aged nineteen during
the Battle of Britain proper and twenty when he was killed.
He was intensely interested in the mechanical side of Spitfires. He knew nearly as much about the Merlin engine as his
engine mechanic, and almost as much about the airframe as
his rigger. He insisted on supervising the harmonization of
his Browning machine guns, whereas I didn't bother and
left it to the armourers — who knew what they were about.
But of course the armourers were delighted with Joe because*

he became one of their team. I should have done it differently; Joe did it as it should be done.

Joe was a great asset to the squadron; lively, humorous, he acted as our disc jockey on the gramophone where the popular tunes of the day were played incessantly when we were not in the air. The broadcast microphone intended to alert the ground crews when the scramble order came was used to send music all round the airfield at high volume. The neighbours must have found their ear-drums pierced with the sound of music; but they also suffered from the noise of our Merlins roaring as the engine mechanics started them up when the scramble order came; and it often came five times a day. Our preference was for Cole Porter, Irving Berlin and Jerome Kern in that order. But Dorothy Lamour was always a favourite, singing sultry melodies about desert islands, which was exactly where we would have preferred to be, not in the skies over Kent.

More than that though, Joe was a poet, although I have no record of his poetry. But when he had enough beer in his belly he would recite impromptu some of the works he had taken such pains to compose. The air, of course, is synonymous with poetry, the wailing spooks, the angels, the billions of souls who make the clouds. I do have one or two examples of poetry composed by airmen and Joe wrote in similar vein. 'What purpose love when death is tomorrow' for example. Or 'time is my murderer, scheduled, punctual, that shall have my bones.' What about 'I have looked over the edge of the world and have seen beyond the fire of the sun, I have found in space so clearly unfurled the mystery that everything is one.'

Anyway, Joe bought it in due course, as he was bound to do. God gave him a little respite by having him shot through the leg by a couple of German bullets and although Joe discharged himself from hospital a few days after the doctors had removed most of the lead, he had only a couple of weeks to live. The Squadron Medical Officer refused to authorize him to fly until the stitches were removed, so Joe had to sulk and write poetry in the interim. His leg was obviously weak when he was allowed off on his first operational sortie after being wounded. I didn't see him go but Buck told me what happened in due course. Buck had climbed at the top cover Messerschmitts but when they scattered, he dived to join in the mêlée at medium altitude. He saw a Spitfire attempting to turn inside a Me 109 and on reflection after landing, he realized that Joe must have been the pilot. The German hit the Spitfire with cannon-fire and probably killed Joe stone dead. Flames spread very rapidly and the Spitfire exploded in front of Buck's eyes. The German was also unlucky because Buck was on to him in a flash, and another Hun bit the dust.

I seem to remember one of Joe's poetic lines but I might have got it wrong. 'Feathering down fretted with golden fire.' Someone else might have written those words, but if the scribe was Joe, then how prophetic it all was.

CHAPTER TWO

BUCK

For a moment I took my eyes off the formation leader, and after a quick glance at the all-enveloping sky, gave my instrument panel the once-over; oil pressure and temperature normal; coolant a bit too hot, but we were climbing fast and it would soon cool down when we levelled out. As I looked at the altimeter the needle floated past the 20,000 ft mark. I was glad I was well wrapped up over my pyjamas, I was grateful for my fleece-lined flying jacket, silk gloves covered by thick gauntlets and wool-lined flying boots.

The three of us had taken off a few minutes before dawn, for the fifth day in succession, in an endeavour to trap a high-flying, early-rising Hun who had been making daily trips to plot the position and course of our merchant convoys. If he were successful his colleagues would then come over later in the day, probably in more difficult weather conditions, and bomb the vessels carrying coal, food and produce down our East Coast from Newcastle to London Docks. Soon we reached our desired altitude of 25,000 ft and commenced our patrol. I was number three in our fairly loose formation – loose so that we could individually devote as much time as possible to searching for our elusive Hun. I looked back just as the round bulge of East-Anglia faded into the mist, but had no idea of the exciting time I was due to have before sitting down to my breakfast of ham and eggs at base.

Suddenly the familiar voice of our senior ground controller rasped in my headphones: 'Red One Buster Squadron, maintain your present course and height. You should see the bandit within a minute.'

Our three aircraft seemed to wobble simultaneously, as we all hunched forward in our cockpits and peered around.

Almost immediately our section leader bawled over the R/T 'Tallyho! Yippee! There he is, at 2 o'clock high.' I looked ahead and a bit to the right, and there he was, a Heinkel III, a few thousand feet above and flying towards us. He saw us almost simultaneously, and turned diving steeply away as fast as he could.

I can't remember my thoughts as I sighted my first Hun. I probably felt a bit sorry for him; he obviously hadn't got a hope against three Spitfires. We went in in order to attack one after the other. My turn came and I lined up my sights on him, but was far too absorbed by the sight of my tracer bullets vanishing into the fuselage to think about breaking away. I saw the rear gunner's gun flashing and winking at me, but his tracer appeared to be passing by just underneath, so I closed right in and didn't break until almost on the point of collision. About to attack again, I noticed that my pals were holding back, and then saw that both the Hun's engines were stopped. He was gliding down to ditch in the North Sea.

The pilot made a nice pancake landing on the water, the crew all piled into a little rubber boat, and the Heinkel slowly sank; we rejoined formation, and set course for base. I couldn't help thinking of those four fellows back there in the little rubber boat. Suddenly, a few miles from the coast, I began to wonder if I was booked for a dip too, because my engine began to choke and splutter, and twin streams of white smoke issued thinly from my exhaust stubs. I scanned my engine instrument carefully – oil temperature, too high; oil pressure, too low; and all at once everything gave way to one thought – I must reach the coast!

I nursed my faltering engine as well as possible, maintaining height with difficulty. Ken and John had pulled to one side, and were escorting me in. 'I thought you were a bit too close to that rear gunner, old boy,' said Ken over the R/T.

I didn't answer. I was relieved to see the coast-line slide under my wing. Now, even if I had to force-land, it would be in a field; all fear of splashing around in the icy ocean had gone. I clattered on and on, watching my tell-tale dials so carefully that I was amazed to find myself almost over our airfield. Was I glad to see it!

I put down my wheels and flaps and was at 500 ft, turning

into the wind to land, when the cockpit filled with clouds of dense smoke. I still had my oxygen mask in position, so I hastily turned the oxygen on to emergency flow, otherwise I should almost certainly have succumbed to the fumes, which were so thick I couldn't see my instrument panel.

Almost immediately – poof! My long-suffering engine caught fire 400 ft from the ground; too low to bale-out, but high enough to provide a few very uncomfortable moments before landing. I side-slipped vigorously to keep the flames from my face and body, skimmed the branches of a tree, sailed straight through a cluster of telephone wires, and landed on the airfield. As soon as I touched-down, the flames became unbearable; I ripped the safety-pin from my harness and dived headlong over the side. Friends watching my involuntary display swear that the aircraft was doing a good 45 mph when I left it.

I landed on my face and chest, the tail plane missed me by inches, the aircraft ran straight on, and I sat up in time to see it swing in a huge arc and turn towards me. I was completely winded and quite helpless, but when about sixty yards away the petrol tank blew up, and the machine collapsed on to its belly, where it burnt itself out, my unused ammunition popping off merrily, effectively keeping the fire brigade at a safe distance.

I recovered my wind, and after a cursory examination found that I was quite intact, with no bones broken. My oxygen mask had saved my face, and my partially inflated Mae West had taken a large part of the shock away from my chest.

I didn't feel quite so sorry for that rear gunner as I watched my aeroplane blazing away, but my feelings softened again as I sat down to a piled plate of ham and eggs some ten minutes later. After all, he had given me something to shoot a line about; for to combine one's first Hun and first crash in the same trip is quite an experience. That little adventure happened on August 8, and before the end of the month I had seen the end of two more Huns – a Messerschmitt 110 and a Dornier.

At that time we were operating from an aerodrome in Cambridgeshire, eating our hearts out for a chance to go south where the blitz was beginning to warm up. In this comparatively quiet area of East Anglia our sole action was provided by solitary bombers and reconnaissance planes, which we usually chased for miles in and out of cloud. We knew that south of the Thames huge formations of bombers and fighters were to be met in clear skies.

We sulked and went berserk because we were kept for so long away from the area where the action was hottest, but our dreams were realized only too soon. Towards the end of August three of us met our last lone bomber, another Heinkel, and shot it down nearly 100 miles out to sea off Great Yarmouth. Then the squadron was ordered to re-deploy to an airfield a few miles south of London, just when the blitz was really beginning.

I have confused memories of our first few days as a front-line squadron in No 11 Group. Somehow I always became separated from the squadron and gambolled along in the sky like a puppy, snapping playfully at huge formations of Jerries, scampering off with my tail between my legs when they turned on me.

Pretty soon I began to settle down. I got used to attacking thirty or forty bombers single-handed, watching Me 109s closing in on my tail, waiting until the last moment before whirling round in a tight turn to engage them. I had incredible luck in that I always seemed to make successful interceptions, but although I sent several down, knowing they would almost certainly crash, I could seldom confirm them as kills; there were always more to deal with and I couldn't spare the time to follow them down and pinpoint the position where they crashed.

Our days lasted from dawn to dusk, roughly ten hours with whirling dog-fights on each occasion, flashing tracer hurtling in the direction of Huns, being shot at, making new friends, losing old ones, snatching brief naps, the letter home: 'Dear Mum and Dad, we are still having a very quiet time here ...' probably written in three parts between patrols! Some of those letters were never finished – instead some of the Mums and Dads read: 'We regret to inform you ...'

Through it all the inevitable record player incessantly blared forth our favourite tunes over the Tannoy speakers around the airfield. Imagine the scene. A dozen youngsters sprawled untidily inside a large wooden hut; some asleep, some playing poker, others reading out-of-date magazines. Occasionally one would pass a remark considered punishable by the rest, whereupon the whole place would be a shambles in a moment – whirling legs and arms, flying cushions – ceasing instantly with the ring of the telephone in the corner of the shack. The nearest pilot would answer. 'Patrol base 25,000 ft'. 'Message received and understood *Buster Squadron Scramble!*'

We would immediately pile out on to the airfield, the waiting ground crews would start up our Spitfires before we were anywhere near them. On with parachute and helmet, into the cockpit, straps on; 'Chocks are away, sir – good luck.' A brief taxi into wind – twelve Spitfires roaring off to come back in two hours' time in ones and twos; not necessarily twelve returned; once only four came back. Some of us may have packed into one sortie the experience of a lifetime.

'O.K. boys, in you go, you know your jobs.'

As the leader's voice crackled in the headphones I turned automatically towards the fighters, the 109s, leaving the bombers to the other sections. I dug my chin into my shoulder and peered to my rear; my tail was clear, but John's – look out, John! For Christ's sake look out!

Oh, hell! Why hadn't he looked out?

I throttled back viciously and turned up and over. The bastard who had got John couldn't pull up in time. He flashed in front of me less than 50 yards ahead. My thumb was ready on the gun button, it seemed to have been there all my life, all my life bullets had been pouring out of those guns – for John.

Now the moment had come. That yellow nose streaked into my sights; I pressed the gun-button; I saw my rounds splashing all along the fuselage of the Messerschmitt, piercing the engine cowlings, shattering his cockpit canopy. Thick clouds of filthy black smoke poured from his engine; he rolled over slowly, so slowly, and I followed him – it – down, watching him disappear into a wood, vertically, at approximately 400 mph.

'There you are, John, fight it out between you. Fight it out either in purgatory or limbo.' As I spoke those words to myself I realized the absurdity of that remark, the stupid bloody-mindedness which had caused it.

My thoughts were cut short. Two more 109s were streaking down hell-for-leather on to my tail. Christ! They saw me

do it; they saw me shoot him down, saw their lovely ⟨
colleague crash, now they are going to kill me for it; b.
had to shoot him down; he shot John down, didn't he? John
was my pal, wasn't he?

Terror, stark terror. They were going to kill me. I was at
their mercy.

Suddenly I saw the tracer flash past. At last here was
something I knew; a concrete form of the Hun's hatred. I
couldn't stop his hatred, but I could dodge his bullets.

Steady, old boy, steady. They've dived from thousands
of feet above; they must be going at twice my speed. I
snapped into a steep climbing turn, they were going too fast
to follow, and I laughed as I saw them go sailing on down.
I laughed – one's moods change quickly in the air – tension –
terror – cool, calm action – relief, all in a second.

I turned down after them, throttle blasted wide open. I'd
show them how to do it.

One of them must have lost sight of me; he zoomed up
again. Good. I didn't have to waste time chasing him. I cut
across the arc of his zoom, stabbed my gun button again –
looked behind . . . Jeez! was there no end to them! Another
was on my tail, coming up fast. I looked in front. My burst
had taken effect. He was scampering away, with a steadily
increasing cloud of black smoke to keep him company.

Pity I couldn't finish him off, but Karl behind me needed
seeing to, and I whirled round, watching his tracer passing
beneath me as I drew away from it. But Karl didn't stay to
argue. He dived and disappeared beneath my wing, and
when I had turned again, he had gone. I was alone in the sky.

*　　　*　　　*

On the afternoon of Saturday, September 7 came the biggest
daylight bomber raid England had ever experienced. Wave
after wave of German bombers attacked London from all
directions, trying to start fires which would guide their night
brothers a few hours later. There were a thousand and more
bombers and fighters in the balbo.

It was about 4 pm and the squadron had been scrambled.
I was washing and shaving, ready for a well-earned twenty-
four hour stand-down when it became evident from the constant mooing of the air-raid sirens that the old Hun was
going it hot and strong. I threw aside the clean shirt I had

been about to put on, and donned instead my dirty old roll-necked pullover and scarf, rushed around to the squadron dispersal, jumped into my Spitfire and took-off to see what I could do. A few minutes later I was over London, at 15,000 feet, with so many enemy formations on either side of me I didn't know which to go for. From then on I can't piece the story together with any clarity.

I attacked time and again, seldom firing my guns, just slicing through the formations in an effort to split them up, doing little or no good, or perhaps a lot of good. There must have been dozens and dozens of British fighter pilots all doing the same thing, all feeling equally lonely.

Suddenly I was surrounded by Me 109s. I saw in my mirror one firing at me from behind; I heard the bullets striking my aircraft; and opened the throttle wide, but there was no response. I half-rolled and dived steeply. They didn't follow. When I was clear of them I checked up; oil pressure, zero; oil temperature off the clock; suddenly my engine seized up and the prop stopped dead. Everything was quiet. I was very angry. A few bullets in the wrong place and I was out of the scrap.

I glided down into the haze, and prepared to make a forced-landing. I was only down to 7,000 ft and had plenty of time. Visibility was shocking, due to industrial smog. I'd have to wait until the last couple of thousand feet before I could select the field where I would have to land. As I watched for a large field, or even an aerodrome, I automatically took all possible precautions. Straps so tight I couldn't move an inch (better than bouncing about like a pea in a pod and breaking my jaw and nose and things); petrol cocks off; ignition off; seat down, in case the Spitfire turned over, which would save a broken neck with luck.

I tried my radio, but it was dead.

Ah! There was a field big enough to land in without doing too much damage to the Spitfire. I lowered my wheels and flaps, and approached to land. Oh, hell! I might have known. It was full of old motor-cars, blocks of cement, and trip wires to stop enemy aircraft from landing for an airborne invasion. By now I was down to 800 ft with no time to pick and choose. I turned away steeply and made for an adjoining small stubble field. As I crossed the hedge a large area of woodland loomed up two hundred yards away. If I landed

with my wheels down I'd probably turn over in the
stubble – a Spitfire isn't a tank. Even if I didn't turn over
I'd certainly still be doing 50 or 60 mph by the time I
reached the woods and would write myself and the aircraft
off. There was nothing else for it. I whipped up the undercarriage, and slapped my Spitfire down on its belly only 100
yards from the trees ahead.

There was an almighty jar; the aeroplane went up on its
nose – I thought it would turn over. But no, it crashed back
on to its tail. Then everything was so still.

I realized I couldn't see. I was in a cloud of smoke. The
damn thing must have caught fire after all. I tore off my
helmet and straps, jumped out, and ran like hell for yards,
with my parachute banging against my backside. I fell and
sat down abruptly, and turned to watch my blazing aircraft,
only to stare amazed at a perfectly sound Spitfire – on its
tummy, yes, but otherwise intact, with a cloud of dry earth
and dust just settling down around it. So much for my fire
scare.

I looked around to see if anyone had seen me doing a
bunk. No, it was all clear. Even if they had, I thought, I have
every excuse; slowing down from 80 mph to a standstill in
about two seconds and as many yards doesn't assist one's
logical thinking.

I got up, walked to the aircraft and picked up my helmet.
It was covered in light-brown dust, and I realized that I was
covered from head to foot in dry earth. I looked at the
damage; my Spitfire had only been struck by about a dozen
bullets, but two or three of them had hit the oil system in
the wrong place; that accounted for my engine failure. Two
men came running wildly across the field, then they stopped,
panting, and looked self-conscious. 'All right, chum?' asked
one. I reassured them. They showed me the way to the nearest telephone and I walked to a farm-house, where a man
and his wife and a sweet little kiddie did all they could for
me. I hoped they didn't think I was rude, but I was in a great
hurry to get away. I wanted to get back to the aerodrome
and take off again but I soon realized it was hopeless. It was
5.15 pm; I'd never be back before dark. I couldn't get
through to my base, so phoned the nearest RAF Station and
gave them particulars; they promised to let my squadron
know, but never did; the next day I was posted as missing.

A policeman arrived, fat and perspiring, in a small car. He seemed excited; when I got to the car I saw why. He had a mixed bag, for my travelling companion was a blond youth, quite handsome, and very pleasant, but a German. We introduced ourselves, and took quite a liking to each other. We held a long conversation in the police station; he had been shot down by a Spitfire, and had baled-out of his 109. We laughingly agreed that the honours were even in our two cases!

He had been particularly unfortunate, for he had received the Iron Cross that very morning. He was 23, and unmarried, very grateful for the bar of chocolate I gave him. We exchanged buttons and badges and addresses. I still have his little badge and address in my wallet. We would communicate after the war.

Soon I had to leave him. A policeman took me on the next stage of my journey back to base. An Irishman, he drove at great speed frequently on the wrong side of the road. He dropped me in a village at 8 pm, and I spent the night there, getting transport from the local aerodrome in the morning. I arrived back at base in the afternoon and the squadron had received no news of me so had given me up for dead. My people had been told I was missing. I soon put that right!

Imagine the party we had that evening; interrupted by the news at 9 o'clock. The announcer's voice came over loud and clear, 'One of our pilots previously reported missing has since returned safely to his unit.'

The drinks were on me.

The morning of September 15 dawned – blue, cloudless sky, fine flying weather; it was Sunday – what of it? Hundreds of German bombers and fighters swarmed over the Channel. Our turn didn't come until about half-past eleven when we were ordered to patrol at 20,000 ft, so off we went.

I was in my usual position as weaver, flying alone 1,000 ft above the rest of the squadron, watching to report and ward off attacks from the rear, or out of the sun. Soon we spotted a formation of Dorniers and the squadron commander led us into the attack. I followed, keeping a keen look-out behind, and wasn't surprised to see a dozen or more 109s diving down on us.

By now the foremost pilots in the squadron were in amongst the Dorniers, so I reported the 109s six o'clock high and engaged the nearest, but before I could get him in my sights I was fairly in the soup; they were all round me. They didn't do their job and protect the bombers, but all went for me, because I was on my own. I saw the squadron disappearing, dealing most effectively with the fleeing Dorniers, and realized that I was in no position to stay and play with a dozen 109s. Several were on my tail, so I beat it, straight down, flat out. I levelled out at 12,000 ft; that shook them off. I was all alone. I called up the squadron on the R/T with the information that I was no longer with them, and beetled off to see what I could find, patrolling a few miles south of London.

I saw a blob coming up from the south, and investigated. Boy! oh, boy! Twenty fat Dorniers materialized, flying wing-tip to wing-tip, ack-ack all round them. I was well ahead and above them, so I shoved the throttle open and dived at them head on. I selected the Hun who appeared to be leading the bunch, settled him in my sights, and let him have it.

There isn't much time to muck about in a head-on attack. I gave a short burst, then slid underneath his big fat belly with only feet to spare, and flashed through the rest of the formation. I hadn't meant to cut it so fine and instinctively ducked as I saw wings, engines, cockpits and black crosses streaking past my cock-pit canopy.

I had reached about 450 mph in my dive, and heaved back on the stick. I blacked out completely as I went up and over in an enormous loop. My vision returned as I lost speed and the centrifugal forces lessened. I was on my back, so rolled over. The speed of dive and pull-out had carried me up ahead of them for another attack. I saw that my first burst had taken effect, the leader had dropped away and to one side, and was in obvious difficulty. The rest of the formation was wobbling about, and didn't seem to know quite what to do. As I dived down again, two Hurricanes turned up and joined in the party. The Huns didn't wait for more, but scattered and fled pell-mell, jettisoning their bombs on open country.

I had helped turn 20 bombers away from London! I yelled and whistled with joy, then pounced on the one I had crippled in my first attack – the Hurricanes were seeing off the others O.K., so I left them to it. He appeared to be having difficulty with one engine, so I fixed that by stopping it altogether. He looked a bit lopsided then, so I stopped the other one too, and he started a long steep glide down.

I saw the rear gunner bale-out, so went up very close and had a look at the aeroplane. It was pretty well riddled. Eight machine-guns certainly make a mess! I had a look at the pilot. He sat bolt upright in his seat, and was either dead or wounded, for he didn't even turn his head to look at me, or watch out for a place to land, but stared straight ahead.

Suddenly a pair of legs appeared, dangling from the underneath hatch; the German navigator I presumed. He got out as far as his waist, then the legs kicked. They became still for a moment then wriggled again, they writhed, thrashed and squirmed. Good God, he's stuck! Poor devil, he couldn't get in or out and his legs, all I could see of them, flailed about wildly as he tried to release himself.

It was my fault. I suddenly felt guilty and almost physically sick, until I thought of the people down below, wives, young mothers, kiddies, huddled in their shelters, waiting for the sirens to sound the All Clear. The legs still wriggled and thrashed, 2,000 ft above the cool green fields, trapped in a doomed aircraft, gliding down with perhaps a dead pilot at the controls. First one boot came off, then the other. He had no socks on, his feet were quite bare; it was very pathetic.

He'd better hurry, or it would be too late.

He hadn't got out when the aircraft was down to a thousand feet. He'd be cut in half when the Dornier hit the ground, like cheese on a grater. In spite of all he stood for, he didn't deserve a death like that. I got my sights squarely on where his body would be, and pressed the firing button. The legs were then still.

The bomber continued on to its destiny. The pilot *was* dead. He made no attempt to flatten out and land, but went smack into a field and the aeroplane exploded. I saw pieces sail past me as I flew low overhead. I didn't feel particularly jubilant.

After a hasty lunch we were back on patrol, and soon ran into loads of bombers. Me 109s were escorting them high above, but they didn't interfere when we attacked. I picked out a Dornier 17 1,000 ft below and dived at him head-on, my favourite way of dealing with bombers. He went into a steep dive and I followed, firing as I caught up on him. The forward gunner returned my fire for a moment and I felt something hit my foot. I found afterwards that it was a spent bullet which had passed through part of my engine, it didn't even go through my flying boot.

Then the return fire stopped. The gunner must have ducked behind his armour plating, or I may have killed him, for as I overtook the aircraft and slid by under the port wing, there was no sign of him and his gun was swinging idly on its mounting. We went into cloud at about 5,000 ft. It was only a thin layer, and as the bomber cleared cloud one of the crew baled-out. The dive grew steeper as the Dornier plunged earthwards. Then, wham! It smacked into a wood and blew up, burning fiercely, setting fire to some of the trees.

I climbed again. After about ten minutes I saw two more Dorniers well below me, flying along together in very tight formation, wings overlapping. I was ahead of them, and down I went in the good old head-on attack, and it got results. They seemed surprised to see me, for they wobbled so violently that their wings touched, and a chunk came off one wing-tip. They both lost height and I gave each of them a quick burst of fire for luck. One was almost on his back as he went into a cloud-layer, the other seemed to be out of control too. I followed them down. We were now just off the coast of Kent. The first went headlong into the drink; there was an almighty splash, and he disappeared.

The second was spinning. There was a piece off one wing. He spiralled crazily down into the water. It reminded me of chestnut leaves in the autumn, fluttering down on to the school playing field. He hit, exploded, and petrol and oil burned fiercely on the surface of the sea. The flames died away; only a few bits of wreckage remained floating.

I then remembered having seen another Dornier explode, and burn – let me see, when was it? Why, only that very morning. It was still Sunday, September 15. The day had been a year.

I flew to the coast, and set course for home. Passing low over fields and villages, rivers and towns, I looked down at labourers working, children at play beside a big red-brick schoolhouse, a bomb crater two streets away; little black heads in the streets, turning to white blobs as they heard my engine and looked up.

I thought of workers in shops and factories, of stretcher-parties and A.R.P. wardens. I hoped the All Clear had gone. I was tired, I'd done my best for them.

* * *

BUCK was given the nick-name Buck because he was a buccaneer. Shades of Francis Drake and Henry Morgan. Buck was tough, strong, almost six feet in height and would have made a champion boxer at his weight if he had been allowed to live. Buck was a strange synthesis; on the one hand he was one of nature's gentlemen; on the other he was a dead-end kid. I doubt if he had seen his twenty-first birthday when he bought it. He would never have gained a commission in the RAF if there hadn't been a war; for one thing he dressed in a very scruffy fashion. None of us dressed quite like the Brigade of Guards when trooping the Colour, mind you, but Buck usually wore a filthy old pullover under his RAF tunic. Further to which it was battered and torn, his scarf positively stank of sweat, which was not surprising as he turned his head around so often to scan the lethal area – about twenty degrees dead astern. What with the stream-lining fairing built into the Spitfire behind the cockpit, and then the armour-plate which protected (protected, what a laugh!) the head and neck, one could only scan in the lethal area by weaving the aircraft around like mad and turning the head so often it nearly came away from the body.

Buck had a bull-neck, a square face, blue eyes, a pushed-in nose and a tough look about him. His hair was fair with a natural curl, he was a womanizer – nothing like as prolific as Randy of course but not too bad. He didn't give a tuppenny damn for anybody and was capable of knocking out a man four stone heavier than himself if the chap annoyed him. He was filled with vibrant energy and whistled almost non-stop. He was most difficult to handle because his sense of discipline was negligible. His self-discipline, on the other hand, was exceptional. I mean, in a single-seater fighter, when you are on your own in the great big sky, no-one can maintain surveillance over your activities. Thus you could do a bunk, fire your guns into the sea, return to base and claim four German aircraft destroyed. Buck never did this. Some chaps did, but none of them, in my view, belonged to Buster Squadron. In theory, the ciné-cameras were proof of claims

40

of German aircraft knocked down. In practice, those cameras worked on only twenty per cent of the necessary occasions. The mechanism broke down, the films were over-exposed, or there was so much ice covering the lenses – no effective heating was applied in 1940 – that there was little evidence of material importance when the films were developed.

Our Intelligence Officer was supposed to reconcile claims with kills, probables, possibles, or merely damaged German aircraft. Our I.O. was a four-letter word. He was an Oxbridge Don, an old man aged about thirty-seven, a cynic, and he refused to authenticate our claims unless he was absolutely satisfied that our target had spun in etc. He always preferred to be given a pin-point of the place where the bandit crashed as this was proof positive in his view. It wasn't in fact. Some of those British pilots who had done a bunk would spot a German aircraft diving to its doom, take note of the hole in the ground and return to base with the information that they had shot down this aerial vehicle and it crashed just there. Buck knew, as I knew, that if we were so half-witted as to dive down from combat altitude after a blazing German wreck just to establish its pin-point on a map, we would thereby lose precious combat altitude. It was an inane system of analysis.

If we had been as stupid as that and then had enough fuel to climb back to combat height, the balbos would more likely than not be back over France and the aircrew of the Luftwaffe would already be laying their French girl-friends in their billets before we had landed back at base. Thus, although Buster Squadron had without doubt an exceptional kill-rate, due to the efforts of our Intelligence Officer we got nothing like the credit we had earned. Other squadrons I.Qs leaned the other way. No-one is ever going to make sense of the kill statistics per squadron unit in 1940.

Buck was an exceptional fighter pilot because of several major factors. In a previous incarnation he had been a cat on a wall. He was also long-sighted. There was only one other pilot on Buster Squadron who had keener eyesight than Buck. His name was Matthew. To see an enemy aircraft before its pilot spots you is the vital, all-important, overriding factor in fighter combat. But then you've got to have veils over your eyeballs which you can close down, because more often than not you are searching the air with

41

the sun blinding you in the process. The sun is a fighter pilot's most deadly enemy. Next in importance is the speed of your reaction when you are, in the enemy's eyes, a dead duck. That's why you must have been a cat before you became a fighter pilot. Finally, you've got to be tough, and also fit. The more gee you can pull over your opponent, the quicker you remove him from two-hundred yards behind your tail and gain a position where you are two-hundred yards behind his tail. It's all to do with turning circles and the ability to withstand high gee forces, which demands that you must be fit.

We normally used Buck as a weaver for several reasons. We had to use weavers, individual pilots turning to and fro above the main squadron formation, because of the crazy formations we used to fly against the deadly, fluid jagdgeschwaders of the Luftwaffe fighters who learned such free-booting tactics in Spain during the civil war. We selected Buck because of his sharp eyesight, because of his extra-sensory perception, because of his cat-like reflexes and because he preferred to be a loner. Captain Albert Ball, VC, DSO, MC, Royal Flying Corps circa 1916, also preferred to be a loner. The Germans, on the other hand, liked it best when they operated en masse – mob-hysteria.

It might be worth-while to embellish this point. In 1940, the fighter pilots of the Luftwaffe in certain important respects, such as weight of armament, were better equipped than those in Fighter Command. Similarly, the Messerschmitt 109 here and there had the edge even over the Spitfire. The direct fuel injection system in the Daimler-Benz engines was superior to our conventional carburettors because they could nose down in a dive, thus applying negative gee, and the engine would continue to function perfectly. Our engines would momentarily cut out if we made any such attempt and our recourse was to half roll and pull back on the stick to go into a dive, thus applying positive gee. Furthermore, for several reasons the Luftwaffe normally held the tactical advantage over us, mainly because of the position of the sun at the time of day when they decided to take the initiative and assemble raids to attack South-Eastern England. On the other hand, German pilots were over hostile territory when they penetrated British air space, whereas we were not; this gave us an advantage in terms of morale, at least, which is the most important factor of them all in aerial fighting.

So you takes your decision and makes your choice as they say. But however it occurred, it always seemed to me that German pilots lacked the utter determination to see the thing through to the bitter end. This is not to say that we were more courageous than they, but I think we were more resolute. I have been involved in dog-fights with German fighter pilots on scores of occasions, and a number of times, when the moment of decision arrived, when the crunch came, many of them virtually threw their hands into the air, gave up the ghost and simply allowed death to penetrate their cockpits. This is quite true if my experience is anything to go by. I used to take particular note of it. It never failed to surprise me.

I always felt confident when Buck was a weaver because I knew he would give us ample warning before belting off on his own. I have not the slightest doubt that Buck shot down approximately twenty German aircraft in 1940. He was credited with merely six! The highest-scoring pilot in 1940, according to the official records, was granted seventeen confirmed kills. If Buck and myself didn't get twenty apiece I would eat my cap.

Buck could never have been my best friend. I am too fay and he was too rough. But I held him in great affection and esteem. The manner of his dying was typical of his every endeavour. He would fly in close formation on German bombers either before or after he had administered the kill. His purpose was to write down on the note-pad he had tied to his thigh the squadron letters, even individual aircraft numbers, of German bombers. Then he would report this information over the R/T to the fighter controller. This was valuable intelligence. It was of great assistance to Air Intelligence who had to assess the Order of Battle and deployment of German squadrons. It was also an extremely hazardous practice but Buck was a brave man. One day, when enormous cu-nimb clouds extended almost from ground level to 40,000 ft, Buck lost his number two on the climb in the turbulence of the black clouds. He later rang up the controller on the R/T and informed him of the squadron letters and individual aircraft number of an He 111. He was probably still in cloud so he must have been flying in very tight formation on the bomber. The gunners could have shot him with their mausers let alone their machine guns at such close range.

That R/T call was the last thing Buck ever did. Then there was silence. A week later a body was washed up in the Thames Estuary which we identified as being Buck's – his identity tag helped in this; but there could be no mistaking the body for the man. The corpse was pretty badly mutilated, apart from being bloated and green from being so long in the sea. I expect the fishes had had a nibble or two. Buck was awarded the Distinguished Flying Cross before he was killed in action. He deserved, in fact, the same range of decorations that Albert Ball gained – VC, DSO, DFC.

Per Ardua ad Astra.

Like Faust, Buck sold his soul to the Devil.

CHAPTER THREE

ALEX

The curtain went up with a vengeance towards the end of May, when 'peacekrieg' became 'blitzkrieg'. Apart from two operational sorties before the fall of Rotterdam, the squadron had seen little action. Following these missions we made two moves in quick succession, remaining at one aerodrome for little over a week. Having landed and refuelled after our last move with no time to spare, one of the flight-commanders went about rounding up the pilots, telling us in hushed tones that we were going places, and advising us to get our small kit packed up and be ready to fly again in ten minutes. During that short space of time we rushed to our quarters in the mess, some of us grumbling about the lack of warning and all the messing around we'd suffered during the past fortnight. A plaintive murmur in colonial English from an Australian pilot on the squadron that 'I shan't be able to write to me wife' made us all burst out laughing, since regularly every day this newly-wed had told his Kate of his love and other sweet nothings. It's funny, but when you are told of an impending offensive action, you all get so keyed-up with the forthcoming sortie that you even become forgetful about the ordinary things of life. It never surprised me to see someone who was turfed out of bed for a sortie at short notice, clamber into his aircraft in his pyjamas having forgotten all about such minor details as donning his flying clothing.

A quarter of an hour later fourteen Spitfires took to the air. Only one or two pilots besides our C.O. knew our destination, and I'm afraid my formation flying left quite a lot to be desired because I tried to keep position on my leader with one eye whilst attempting to survey the ground below with the other, trying to work out our route. Eventually after much speculation we touched down at Kenley, south of London.

We quickly refuelled and took off for Martlesham Heath, only ten minutes flight-time away.

On landing I saw on the airfield more Spitfires than I had hitherto imagined it was possible to park. After a conference between the flying leaders, the word was passed around that we were to sweep the Dunkirk area in protection of the evacuation of the British Expeditionary Force. Our squadron was chosen to act in the top cover role above three others. We were to fly at 26,000 ft. Before take-off I found that the valve on the oxygen bottle would only turn with the greatest of difficulty. These things normally don't worry me much, but the tense state of mind I was in made me over-react and I lost my temper. However the ground crew sorted the snag out.

At last with a thunderous roar we all took off and sorted out our respective positions in formation. I saw nothing of the other three squadrons after we arrived over the English coast, because I was busy keeping station and also a sharp look-out. To be precise, I saw nothing during the whole sortie. It was a completely uneventful trip apart from a chilly feeling where my feet ought to have been. My squadron commander had us quite perturbed on the return flight from Dunkirk, during which time I saw only sea, and plenty of it; and a low fuel gauge reading didn't exactly promote a contented frame of mind. It was damn funny really, on reflection, to see the whole squadron open out of formation on crossing the English coast, in failing light and poor visibility, every one trying to be the first to establish our position and sight our base. The trip cost us one aeroplane when the pilot's undercart failed to come down, resulting in a sensational tearing noise as terra firma grabbed at his fuselage.

We flew two sweeps over Dunkirk the following day. These were flown at 25,000 ft and above. I saw nothing, but other pilots in the wing were engaged in combat. I suppose we served our purpose by giving some protection to the British Army, but I was not entirely convinced of that.

The ground crews worked all night servicing our Spitfires when we landed back at dusk. Further squadrons flew into the airfield at dawn the next day. There were aeroplanes to the right, aeroplanes to the left, aeroplanes in front, in fact there were as many fighters as the airfield could contain. The various commanders of the participating squadrons had

46

visited the Ops. Room where the general plan was outlined to them, and my squadron commander briefed us on his return, giving us the tactical doctrine – if any. We took off in vics of three aircraft. Joe was No. 2 on the right, with myself on the left as No. 3 of our section which was led by a daring and experienced Flying-Officer. We were in Green Section and brought up the rear of the four sections which comprised the squadron. We were very quick to take up our position. We gained height circling the aerodrome; we had been told to set the fuel flow to the Merlins at weak mixture to conserve our fuel, and also be sparing with oxygen. The other three squadrons comprising our wing of four units slowly got into position on the climb.

The intention was to cross the English coast at 7 a.m., all stationed correctly at our pre-arranged heights – 27,000 ft for us. The actual sweep over French soil was to last an hour, since our fuel supply wouldn't leave us a good fighting margin if this period were exceeded. Whilst we were gaining height, I found myself doing the routine things such as trimming the aircraft to fly nicely to the hand, adjusting the seat and straps for safety and comfort, setting the gunsight, and switching on the necessary heaters which were supposed to neutralize the cold experienced at high altitude. I was very apprehensive. Would we meet anything this time? I wondered if the Jerries were as crafty as we thought they were in using the sun and extra height. Anyhow I'd much rather be up above the ground than one of those poor blighters on the beach at Dunkirk. I visualized the morning papers of the past few days, each prominently displaying a map of the battle area, the same area to which we were heading, and each showing a complete encirclement of the Dunkirk locality by German armoured divisions.

After about 20 minutes flight time across the North Sea, the dial registering my oxygen content in the cylinder suddenly showed an abnormally large drop on the gauge on my instrument panel. I immediately appreciated that there must be a leak somewhere in the system, and it was odds on that my oxygen supply would run out on me. However, I elected to carry on until it really did get empty, and I proceeded to use a supply equivalent to a height of 5,000 feet below that at which we were flying in an attempt to economize on oxygen. It gave me a slight headache for a short while, but an occasional burst of the correct quantity seemed to overcome that.

I saw nothing of the other squadrons or any other aircraft outside Buster Squadron as we swept over the North Sea and carried out our patrol, and I was watching the oxygen gauge very carefully. After about fifty minutes on patrol it was down on the red danger mark, indicating that it was almost empty. Without oxygen at 27,000 ft I would pass out in a very short time. I was about to call up my C.O. for permission to return home, when someone suddenly spotted German aircraft far below and the C.O. put us into a dive, thus solving my problem of lack of oxygen supply.

At about 12,000 ft we saw several batches of bombers – He 111s and Ju 88s – sweeping around the area of Dunkirk. My section leader manoeuvred in order to attack five Ju 88s which appeared to be oblivious of our presence. Flak came up from the ground but we ignored it. In order to see my selected target, a Ju 88, I had to rub my windscreen continually with my gauntleted hand as the forward view was completely obscured by ice. I rubbed clear a small patch sufficient to see through, but I had to keep rubbing as the frost formed again as quickly as I removed it. It's a sod holding the joy-stick in one hand and rubbing away with the other. If you don't keep scanning to your rear you might be jumped, but how can you scan when the cockpit canopy is covered in hoar-frost? And how can you sight your guns with a frosted-up windshield? However, I managed to take a bead on one of the Junkers, following which, as I saw it, I caused jets of flame and black smoke to trail from its engines; it was certainly badly damaged if not destroyed in the air. Our leader broke off the attack sideways and downwards in the approved fashion, with No. 2 and myself following in close attendance, then he climbed again to position us for a further attack. I wondered what was being said and done in the bomber meanwhile.

It was while I was trailing in this climb that I spotted a silver Messerschmitt 109 circling into position to have a crack at me from the rear. Giving the others a yell over the R/T, I wheeled away into a hard turn to port which appeared too much for him since he sheered off at maximum speed. Then all of a sudden plumes of white smoke began streaming back past my cockpit canopy, emanating from my engine exhaust stubs. I had probably been hit by German or French flak. A quick glance at the instruments gave me the information that the engine really had good reason to be as rough as it felt. When black smoke and oil fumes suddenly enveloped me from under my feet, blotting out everything and almost suffocating me, I realized that I was in dire trouble.

After a struggle I hauled the hood back against the vacuum effect of the slip stream. This action served to drive all the smoke and filth back to the bottom of the cockpit and cleared my head a bit. I switched off the engine to decrease the risk of fire and a petrol-tank explosion; then assuming a nice gliding speed and performing a series of gliding turns, I surveyed the earth below for a suitable landing-ground. The beach first sprang to mind, but this was definitely out. Every few yards was littered with wrecked lorries and the general debris of war. The sea I didn't relish, as I thought the chances of rescue would be remote. The various fields in France looked uncommonly small and dangerous from 6 – 7,000 ft, so my only alternative was to bale out. I had just removed my helmet and released my safety harness when, as luck would have it, I caught sight of a Messerschmitt and the pilot must have realized I was a sitting duck. He closed in on my tail from above to port. With no engine there was only one thing I could do. A sharp diving turn brought me straight into the huge pall of black smoke which stretched up to nearly 5,000 ft from the blazing oil tanks in the Dunkirk docks area. When I emerged into sunshine again on the other side of the smoke, my friend Fritz in the 109 had disappeared.

When I was about 2,000 ft, and with the airspeed of 180 mph, I started to abandon aircraft in the manner so often discussed and recommended in the pilot's room. The idea was to turn the aircraft on to its back, then drop out, pulling the rip-cord at one's own convenience. The thing which hadn't been stressed, but which proved the most important, was that the safety harness should remain fastened until the last moment, when, on extracting the release-pin, gravity (according to the venerable Mr. Newton) should assist exit.

As I've already explained, the harness which should have been tight was already off. As a result, in attempting to invert the machine, I found myself three-quarters of the way out and unable to move. A very chaotic state of mind prevailed. However, a fortunate lapse of memory excludes the hectic activity of the next few seconds. I have a vague remembrance of making two attempts to push myself out, and the next thing I knew I was floating down under an enormous silk canopy.

When I landed on the end of my parachute I hurt my back. British troops rescued me and I was ferried back to Harwich and put in hospital for a month or more. In due course, when the doctors thought I was fit enough, I returned to Buster Squadron which had, by now, moved down to the 11 Group area, South of the Thames, adjacent to London. When I saw the boys I had quite a shock. They looked tired and some of them had been wounded. Three chaps had baled-out, six had been killed. It was worse than that in retrospect and it left a mark. The squadron's score had been just about trebled. I discovered that I had a new flight-commander in Bill, but he then had the misfortune to get shot-up and burned before baling-out, so I took over command of the flight. The Huns had been coming over in large raids, almost three times a day. Up we went the following morning and after a short patrol enemy aircraft were sighted. We flew towards them and as we neared them someone bawled over the R/T that we were being jumped by a gaggle of Messerschmitts.

I looked around and couldn't see anything, but the squadron was splitting up and going hell-for-leather towards the bombers. Suddenly a flaming object which I recognized as a Me 109, blazing from wing-tip to wing-tip, flashed past a hundred yards in front of my nose. This shook me not a little, and from that point on the sky was black with aircraft. Yet I seemed very much alone, the twisting, turning aircraft all around seemed to my unaccustomed eyes to be all German, although, of course, they weren't. I then recognized a Heinkel bomber flying home. I went after him, out for the kill so to speak, but I was suspicious. I whipped around to have a look-see at my tail, and sure enough there was a Me 109 closing range fast, diving from above. From that position I didn't stay to argue but dived vertically away.

On the next sortie I had a couple of bursts with the Brownings but I didn't hit anything. The following afternoon, however, we again made an interception and I succeeded in shooting at a couple of Heinkels, but I was attacked by 109s and dived away. Then I was delighted to see a Dornier 17 just crossing the coast below me at 9,000 ft. I gave the fuselage a burst, then I belted away at the Dornier's starboard engine which erupted in flames. I gave the port engine the rest of my ammunition and the Dornier vanished into cloud.

I then observed smoky streaks passing my starboard wing, I looked in my mirror and saw a 109 attacking. I was in a nasty position and had run out of ammunition; accordingly I faded into cloud vertically. Some 2,000 ft lower I burst through cloud just out to sea off the coast. As I straightened out I noticed a glow in the cloud nearby and the Do 17, obviously the one I had shot at, came tearing through, diving almost vertically with both engines on fire. The bomber hit the sea and disintegrated about six miles from the coast. My previous score being one-third of Heinkel, I now had more than doubled that. I returned to the airfield greatly elated, life wasn't too bad after all.

On September 15, 1940, on the first of that day's raids on London, I'm practically certain we were the first squadron to intercept. I was leading Buster Squadron's look-out section and I was responsible for attempting to ward off initial attacks by German fighters on the squadron. All of a sudden the squadron got mixed up in a mêlée just as we were trying to engage the bombers. While climbing up above the dog-fight I was attacked by a 109, but luckily I saw him start his attack, so I waited as long as I dared and then hauled the Spitfire round. This manoeuvre had two reasons for its execution – firstly, to avoid being hit, and secondly with a vague idea of getting on the 109's tail in the process. However, he was going far too fast and I couldn't catch him; he went into cloud and I followed, hoping to get him underneath, but when I came out of the cloud he was nowhere to be seen.

Knowing then that I was out of the fight, I started back home, cruising at only 2,000 ft. It was then I saw some bursts of ack-ack fire so I turned and saw a Dornier 17 climbing towards the cloud. I could scarcely believe my eyes and good fortune. I attacked and saw my bullets going home. As I broke away from this attack I saw two of the crew bale-out. I went again to the attack and this resulted in the pilot and another German baling out; the Flying Pencil went spiralling on down and crashed in someone's back garden in Rochester.

One evening, three days later, we were airborne as part of a two-squadron wing on patrol, and happened to run into a bunch of 109s at almost the same height. There was high cirrus cloud around at this altitude, and I did not see the bombers which these Messerschmitts were escorting in the high-cover role. However, our co-squadron dealt with the bombers, and as we swept off to attack the 109s they climbed for the cloud. George, who was leading the squadron, chased one; I was leading the second section, and when the squadron began to split up I followed George but couldn't keep up with him, so I went after another Hun.

My number two maintained formation on me, so I knew my tail was O.K. I climbed from behind and beneath the 109. Eventually I was about in range and calculated that he obviously had not seen me, so, holding my fire, I crept right in, giving two bursts from just behind him. The first knocked bits off the aircraft and the second squirt sent some incendiaries into his petrol tank. The whole issue went up in flames and the pilot baled-out pretty darned quick.

I inadvertently stalled and dived away; my number two, Jim, the old bloodhound, kept up with me, and we saw nothing else. Even the bombers had disappeared. Coming down to 15,000 ft we noticed some ack-ack bursts out to sea; as we watched, the flak moved overland and then stopped. Shortly afterwards we saw four fighters fading in and out of the haze. Jim yelled out when he saw them, so up we climbed into the haze, and saw them come out of this about 200 ft above us. They were Me 109s so in we sailed, guns belching, whereupon they broke into pairs, two crossing above me and tackling Jim. I went for the others. My two Me 109s broke up, one diving down; I got a lovely sight on him but hell, I had left the button on 'Safe'. I hastily put it in the Fire position and then managed to squirt at the other 109, I saw lumps fly off him, including one of the famous 109 tailplane struts, then I observed tracer coming past from behind.

I didn't need to ask what that meant, so I blacked myself out as I pulled the gee as hard as I could. It was effective but after that I had no idea where everything was or where

Jim had got to. I could see no sign of my winged bird, and didn't know whether he had been able to get back home. Five minutes after landing I was relieved to see Jim joining the circuit; he landed and said he'd got one of his 109s in flames. Shortly afterwards we were released for the day, and we went off to the pub in celebration of what we, anyway, called a successful day.

I think I can honestly say that October 20 provided the most exciting hour of my young life. We were sent off on our usual after-breakfast patrol, hiccoughing away with that awful mixture of a hastily swallowed fried egg and pure oxygen. After cruising around for nearly an hour at over 30,000 ft, the squadron sighted flak bursts at our own height on our starboard side. The enemy aircraft were below us, and we recognized them as Me 109s. They were flying head on towards us and we for once were in that lovely position above and up-sun. We came down and into the attack, and then it was a case of making one's personal selection.

My Hun must have spotted me because before I could get in range he went into a vertical dive; the 109 has *some* good points, and diving is definitely the best. I followed him and found that with almost pathetic slowness I was over-taking him and I held my fire until I was in range. We had gone down so fast and were flying at such speed that my controls would hardly move even when I used all my strength on the control column. I was almost certain we were quite out of the rest of the dog-fight, and that no other nasty-minded Jerry could interfere with me, but I was wrong, wildly wrong.

Having got within range of my target, I was literally just about to press the gun button when there was a hell of a crash and thump on my aircraft. It was the unmistakable heralding of a cannon shell, and I counted five more in quick succession. Owing to the high speed I couldn't take very quick evasive action, and in any case I soon found that I had no elevator-control at all. The Hun's pal had definitely got me. The aircraft went into a steep left-hand climbing turn and for a little while afterwards, owing to the colossal pressure, I just blacked-out completely. I tried to lift my hands to open the hood, but I couldn't. I put the stick in every position, but it seemed to have absolutely no effect; I aged by ten years. The engine seemed to howl more and more, and then I gave in. I thought goddamit and I'd nearly got him; well, it's been a grand life; bit short though; wish the Spitfire would hurry up and hit the ground; can't bear the suspense.

Then the pressure eased off, the blackout wasn't so dense; my one prayer was that I should regain my faculties looking at blue sky and not mother earth; then I'd be going up and not down. There we are – yes, blue sky – relief number one. I tugged at the hood release but with no result; tugged again, same thing; then one more bloody great wrench and it flew open – relief number two. Flames from the oil tank were bouncing about in the corner of the cockpit, and spurred me to greater efforts. I tore the safety harness release ring, stood up in the cockpit only to find I'd forgotten to unravel my helmet, and was still fastened to the aircraft. Ducking back out of the slipstream I actually tore the leather of the helmet as I wrenched it off. (I found the helmet later and was amazed at the strength I must have used to tear it like that). I stood up in the slipstream, again leaning slightly to the left, and, hey presto, the wind plucked me out – relief number three.

Jesus! expresses my impression and thoughts in one word. I fell like a stone through the air and the air cooled my face and ears. Take it easy – don't fumble – hands seem frozen – where's that blasted ring? – got it! A sharp pull on the rip-cord and a jerk – parachute open – relief number four. But how had it opened? Not correctly. My left foot was caught up in the silk cords and I was upside down. Knowing that it wouldn't be the nicest way to make contact with the soil of Kent, I climbed up the other side of the parachute, hand over hand, and after a short struggle, managed to free my foot – relief number five. Dropping into a more or less right way up position I became conscious of utter silence save for the spasmodic rattle of machine-gun fire and howl of engines, in the battle still going on far overhead. Then I was aware of the loud, wheezing, semi-choking noises coming from me as I gulped in air for the first time, it seemed, since we started the attack on the Huns. Looking around I then realized that the parachute wasn't properly open. The shoulder-straps, instead of holding me behind the shoulder-blades, were tangled together, chafing my ears. Farther up some of the cords were crossed, and I realized that the silk canopy was not fully open, consequently I was falling considerably faster than I should have been. Struggle as I might, I could not improve the position. I glanced at the second hand of my wrist-watch and wondered what time it would take to hit the ground. There was a cloud below me so I thought I'd do a practise landing on it to time just how fast I was falling. Judging by the rate at which I passed through that cloud I was going pretty fast, too fast for safety let alone comfort. I afterwards discovered that the cloud was at 7,000 ft, and I reckon I couldn't have been less than 27,000 ft when I was shot-up. I guess I got out at about 11,000 ft, so I must have dived the Spitfire some 16,000 ft while blacked-out.

Floating down in this extremely uncomfortable position, I saw a town beneath me and prayed I would land in a tree to break my fall. Gradually I drifted south-west, occasionally breaking into a swing and twisting slowly round on the end of the parachute. Soon I had the impression that I was falling very fast as I got lower; it now seemed that I was not stationary in mid-air. I tried to judge where I would strike the ground, but trees seemed far away from my point of destiny. The ground came nearer and nearer with terrifying speed. I saw a farm yard and faces gazing at me. Down to about 500 ft and over some high-tension cables, which, even though I was several hundred feet above them, made me instinctively lift my feet up. I then appreciated that I was going to land in not just a tree, but a whole wood – relief number six.

Just above the topmost branches I covered my face with my arms to prevent my eyes being torn to shreds. My feet hit the tree with great crashing noises and I found myself swinging between a couple of trees like a human yo-yo. The canopy had caught in the interlocking branches of the two trees, and I was in mid-air. Those trees were tall, they were of the type with no lower branches to catch hold of, I was twenty feet up and almost over an asphalt road, so I couldn't release the harness and drop without fear of further injury. I observed a small branch sticking out from one of the trees out of reach, so then I did a Tarzan stunt, swinging back and forth until I gained enough momentum to grab the twig. Gingerly pulling myself in, praying it wouldn't break, I reached the trunk, scrambled up into the branches, released the harness and lay there panting.

Farmers, housewives, errand boys and Home Guard all arrived at once on the road beneath, doubting my nationality, but my language seemed to convince them I couldn't be other than British. The Home Guard gallantly made a human ladder for me, sitting on each other's shoulders, and a minute or so later I touched the earth. I felt sick, and was rescued by a Squadron-Leader who had followed me, as I floated down, in his car. He produced a flask of brandy. As I was taken off to a hospital for the once-over, I felt my real self for the first time for a good twenty-five minutes – final relief.

*　　　*　　　*

ALEX was a yeoman of England. He originated from Lancashire and a lot of Norman conquerors finished up in that county, so I suspect that Alex was basically an aristocrat even though he was nominally a yeoman. One had to listen very carefully to recognize the slight touch of Lancashire accent when Alex spoke because, on the face of it, his accent approximated to Oxbridge. Alex was an exceptional fighter pilot, keen of eye, sharp with his reflexes, although slightly too tall for the ideal specification. He had learned to be a fighter pilot on the Gauntlet biplane, which wasn't a bad method of achieving one's diploma. He certainly knew how to shoot straight, I should know. One day we were flying as a pair and he blew the cockpit canopy off a Messerschmitt 109 from 400 yards – almost extreme range for our puny batteries of eight .303 in Browning machine-guns. It exploded and we both had to get the hell out quick sharp to avoid the airborne debris which was coming straight towards us. I think he only used about 20 rounds per gun, about a half-second burst, on that occasion. That was nice shooting, very good marksmanship in fact.

Alex was tough, broad shouldered, red of face, with good hands and a wide grin which exposed teeth of purest white. He was not an intellectual, but nevertheless, as he was a regular RAF officer, he would have finished up as an Air Marshal had he been allowed to live.

Alex was certainly an artist in his ability to shoot down German aircraft and this is a very complex business. Either one has to be a mathematician or a natural marksman. A great number of complicated factors become involved.

Alex overdid it eventually. He threw all his energy into beating up the Luftwaffe, despite the fact that they sometimes nearly beat him into small shreds. He became so weary in the course of time that he forgot certain vital actions such as putting his undercarriage down prior to landing. He belly-landed three perfectly serviceable Spitfires because prior to landing he forgot to move the lever which slid the undercart down. This went on well into 1941 and he joined Buster Squadron in about 1938. It had nothing to do with drink because he only sucked back a couple of pints of beer of an evening; it was purely and simply caused by battle-weariness or combat fatigue. I was greatly worried by this but, at the time, I was in no position to have him sent off on rest from operations. He had already been awarded the DFC, was well on the way to warrant a bar to his DFC, and the French Government in exile had given him the Croix de Guerre. He had no life outside fighter operations, he would have become a zombie if he had been sent for a rest period as an instructor.

I think that Alex began to realize all this. I also believe that he then got a fixation which amounted to a kind of death-wish. Somehow he could never work out how the war would end, he didn't realize that Hitler would be stupid enough to invade Russia or that America would intervene as Britain's ally. He felt, I think, that he had done his job in defending British air space in 1940, that the Luftwaffe were now beginning to make a hash of their operations by day and there was nothing really left to live for. In my opinion, Alex performed a kamikaze operation: he committed suicide by taking on overwhelming odds.

The sequence of events only became known when the archives of the Luftwaffe were exposed to British analysis after the war ended, but we had a glimmer of realization at the time, gleaned from radar plots and so on. Alex detailed himself to fly across the English Channel on a weather reconnaissance mission and there was nothing unusual in that – I used to fly such sorties frequently. The radar operators watched him cross the Channel and then lost him. A little later, however, they saw signs of Luftwaffe activity. I gained this information by researching the logs of the radar operators. I checked it all out after the war with the assistance of the operational analysis people and the picture clarified in my mind.

Alex flew over Cap Gris Nez and hit at a Luftwaffe airfield in a strafing attack. He then proceeded on to another and did likewise. It seems that he destroyed twelve aircraft on the ground in these attacks. This must have meant that he turned and had several other goes at each airfield, which was hazardous as the flak gunners would have been waiting for him after they recovered from their initial surprise. He was shot down by flak over the second airfield and his Spitfire disintegrated in a plume of black smoke. They dug out his Spitfire which had fallen into a bog and was buried twenty feet under the sod. They put what remained of Alex in a biscuit tin and weighted the coffin with sand-bags.

But at least they gave the biscuit tin a Christian burial.

CHAPTER FOUR

MATTHEW

It was at the beginning of the blitz when I joined Buster
Squadron, and after about twenty operational hours' flying
and never having seen a Jerry, I was rather browned-off,
but I knew the day was coming, and when it came I had
one of the most exciting times of my life. We were stationed
at an aerodrome on the coast of East Anglia; our work
consisting mainly of acting in protection of convoys and
sometimes an interception patrol. We slept in the dispersal
hut, because we came to readiness at dawn, which was about
4.30 a.m. and usually did not finish until 11.30 p.m. with an
hour off for breakfast, lunch and dinner, if we were lucky.

One bright summer afternoon our section was ordered off
to patrol the East Coast from point X to point Y. We had
climbed to 25,000 ft when I sighted an aircraft flying towards
us about 3,000 ft above. I immediately informed the leader
over the R/T and said I would lead the section towards it
as it was outside his vision. As soon as he saw the aircraft,
which we identified as a Dornier 17, he took the lead again
and ordered the section to prepare to attack. The section
climbed above the Dornier and the leader put us into line
astern formation. We then dived in an astern attack, and as
my section leader closed range the rear gunner of the bomber
opened fire, which did not seem to be very accurate; it seems
that the German rear-gunner was killed when my leader
opened fire. Then number two attacked; by this time another
gunner had taken his position in the tail of the Dornier and
number two received a hail of return fire. When he had
finished firing, the Dornier's port engine was in flames and its
fuselage had had pieces knocked off. Then I attacked,
opening fire at about 250 yards swiftly closing range.
Suddenly the German bomber's starboard engine caught

fire; its oil was thrown back by the slipstream on my windscreen and I could no longer see out of the cockpit. I immediately put on full left rudder, at the same time I pushed the control column over to the left and did not level out until I had lost 2,000 ft in height.

As my cockpit canopy was also covered with oil I decided to open it, and much to my surprise saw the Dornier about ten feet away on my starboard side. The rear gunner played merry hell into my machine with his machine-gun before I could break away. My cockpit canopy departed, the radio was put out of action and I decided that no Jerry was going to get away with this, so I attacked again, but this time I opened fire at 100 yards, not stopping until I noticed that my own engine was on fire. Under these conditions I had to break upwards to gain as much height as possible, which would allow extra time to study my position before force-landing.

I now had only 5,000 ft between me and the sea, the coast was about ten miles away, my engine had cut out, the glycol was on fire, and my wireless out of action. Should I bale-out, or should I try and glide as near the coast as possible? Then I noticed a lightship below me. In a flash I made up my mind that I would try and land my machine in the sea by the side of the lightship rather than bale-out, as the wind might carry me farther out to sea.

Having decided on this line of action, I glided towards the lightship, thinking my troubles were over. Were they hell! Actually they had only just started. The sea was quite rough and I could not see anything to tell me which direction the wind was blowing from, so I had to take a chance and I wondered what would happen if my airspeed indicator failed to work on the way down. I am now sure that if it had failed I would not be here to write these lines. I believe that this was the only instrument that I looked at all the way down. I could not see anybody on the lightship. By this time I was only about 500 ft up and I had great trouble in judging my altitude vis a vis the sea. Instead of pancaking on the surface, the Spitfire stalled, the port wing dropped and hit the sea with a hell of a crash, and I was thrown forward with great force.

This was the last thing I remember until I recovered consciousness a few seconds later. I was still in the cockpit, the Spitfire was beginning to dive towards the sea-bed and the water in the cockpit was by now up to my neck. I took a deep breath as I was dragged under by the aircraft. After struggling I freed the harness and tried to push myself clear of the machine, but my parachute caught on a jagged edge of the torn fuselage. I gave a hefty kick and managed to get clear of the machine. As I had been under the water for quite a time now, I was beginning to feel dizzy and I had visions of my name being on the RAF casualty list, killed in action; and of a telegram arriving at home informing my parents I had been bumped off. Suddenly all this thinking stopped, as I slowly ascended and reached the surface, took a deep breath and once again I felt fairly normal. The sea was rough and I could see damn all, but at last I spotted the lightship about 200 yards away up-current, and started to swim. After about 50 yards I realized that I still had my parachute on. I had also forgotten to blow up my Mae West.

After discarding my parachute, I again made for the lightship, but my flying boots seemed to drag so I took them off, then I realized I still hadn't blown up my Mae West. I tried to do this but did not seem to have any effect. Then I noticed that the air was coming out of the side where there were two holes. Hell! They had been made by a bullet and only just missed my body. I think I would have died of shock had I not been so cold. By now I was beginning to wonder whether I would ever reach the lightship; I did not seem to get any nearer and I was feeling the effects of my submarine activities.

The current was rather strong and I was getting weak. As the lightship was still deserted I concluded it worked automatically, but suddenly the lightship became alive with men dashing about, so I yelled like hell and in about a minute a boat was lowered and started to come towards me and I just floated in the sea and waited. When it got within ten yards I heard a sailor calling, 'We're coming, mate,' but another of my rescuers was not so sure. He said, 'It's a bloody Hun, Bill. Give me the boathook just in case he gets annoying.' Bill answered, 'No! He came in a Spitfire, Curly.' As the boat got nearer I saw a tough-looking seaman standing in the stern with a vicious-looking boathook in his left hand. Suddenly I sprang to life and yelled a few words of old-fashioned English. It worked like a miracle. The seaman dropped his boathook (maybe he was shocked) and the rest of the crew cheered. The tough-looking seaman once again had something in his left hand. Ah! a bottle of rum; and I needed some of it.

After the Trinity House men had got me aboard the lightship they took down all my particulars and sent out a W/T message to shore. I then stripped my wet clothes off and had a bath. By this time I was beginning to feel seasick so I dashed to the side, but forgot about it when I noticed a destroyer coming towards the lightship and also two other light naval craft just arriving from Harwich harbour ten miles away. Considering they arrived only fifteen minutes after I had pancaked on the water, I have no fear of rotting in the sea in future when I know that we have such an efficient Navy to look after us.

After thanking everyone on the lightship and by request handing over my Mae West, flying suit, lapel badges, and many other oddments as souvenirs, I left. The skipper had given me chocolate and cigarettes. At last I was on my way back home. When the lifeboat was alongside the destroyer I was attached with slings and hauled on board. As soon as I was out of the water but still being hauled on board, the destroyer was under way. Once on board the destroyer I was taken to the bridge and the captain shook hands with me and I again gave my particulars. He then gave me his cabin, and the ship's doctor had a good look at me and much to my surprise decided to stitch my head; I had no idea it was cut; he also gave me a few injections. When I had been lying down for about ten minutes I felt very tired and went to sleep. A little later I woke up feeling extremely unsafe, and in the distance I heard a gun fire and then another. Gradually the guns got nearer and nearer, until there was a hell of a crash above me. I sat up immediately and hit my head on the deck above, then I collapsed on my bed again. I was sure by now that the ship was being attacked or had hit a mine or something. Then the door opened and in walked the doctor who informed me that it was only a 4-inch gun on deck practising. The other gunfire was from destroyers in line astern behind ours.

We put into Sheerness at 6 a.m. the following morning and it had been arranged that I should be transferred to a hospital at Chatham. At 8 o'clock I got up and had some breakfast. Afterwards I sat in a deck chair on the quarter-deck, but at 9.30 a.m. the air-raid sirens sounded and about 100 enemy aircraft arrived overhead. The ack-ack fire was so tremendous that the raid was completely split up and only a few aircraft managed to dive-bomb the harbour. For the next five minutes the noise was colossal – the whistle of falling bombs, crashes as bombs exploded in the water and 4-inch ack-ack guns opened fire; all this was mingled with the rat-tat of machine-guns and pom-poms. The destroyer seemed to rock once or twice when the bombs fell near, but nothing was sunk and about ten German aircraft fell into the estuary.

I was driven to a naval hospital by a smashing Wren and put to bed. The hospital staff were tremendous and my nurse was a wizard type. The naval doctors were most kind and for five days I had the most enjoyable time imaginable, but I was getting home-sick for my squadron. I had already learned that they had moved to 11 Group, right in the front-line.

The leader and No. 2 of my section had not seen me crash and were very surprised to find that I had not returned. Nobody received any message until three hours later, but when it arrived they gathered that I was on a cruiser and would not be back for a few weeks. The C.O. was astonished when I arrived back, but he would not let me fly. The squadron doctor then sent me on two weeks' leave, which did not do me much good as I stayed in London for a week and went on the booze. Then I returned to the squadron, but the squadron commander sent me away again as I was not yet fit enough to fly. I spent most of my time in cinemas as there was not much else to do. My relatives were so good to me that I got fed up with them, and was relieved to get back to the squadron. I arrived back there and learned that the Dornier which shot me down had crashed a few miles from the lightship.

The blitz was at its height when I returned. The squadron looked different with DFCs on several pilots' uniforms and parts of Me 109s with swastikas littered all over the squadron dispersal. But all I wanted to do was to get my own back. The first time up after my crash there were six of us on patrol when we sighted about thirty Me 109s about 5,000 ft above us, so we climbed to attack, but we were then jumped by another thirty Messerschmitts from behind. I was attacked by six at once, but after being hit three times I managed to get away by going into a spin.

After spinning from 25,000 ft to 5,000 ft I pulled out. All the time I expected to get a few more bullets in my Spitfire because I did not then realize that German fighter pilots tended not to follow Spitfires and Hurricanes down once they went into a spin or a vertical dive. Much to my surprise, however, I saw a Me 109 about 400 yards ahead of me flying south. I closed to 200 yards and opened fire. It dived and the last I saw of it was when it entered cloud at 2,000 ft with glycol flames pouring out of the radiator, but I could only claim it as damaged. When I got back to the base two of the boys had not arrived back but they arrived later, each having shot down a Me 109. The total score for this fight was six 109s shot down, three probably shot down, and four damaged. Our only casualty was my machine, which was repaired in not very many days. After a few more operational sorties over London and the south coast I began to feel at home fighting 109s.

On October 10 the squadron was ordered to scramble, but unfortunately I was held up because my Spitfire went unserviceable, so I had to take off later by myself. After searching for the squadron I called up the ground station and they told me that the squadron was involved in a bloody great dogfight and if I flew down to the coast I might meet with German aircraft returning home. I climbed to 35,000 ft and waited. At last I saw six Me 109s in line astern, crossing the coast between Dover and Folkestone. I dived and opened fire. I was out of range and my fire merely warned them that I was attacking. They spread out fanwise, making it very difficult for me to attack any one of them without then finding the other five on my tail, so I dived for cloud cover. Once in the cloud I decided to stalk them over the Channel. I hopped in and out of the clouds, gradually catching them up, but I did not realize that by this time I was over Calais until my Spitfire rocked when Jerry sent up about 100 flak shells. Unfortunately one piece of shrapnel pierced my radiator and my engine seized up. I wondered if I would have to make another forced-landing in the sea and if I did whether I would be as lucky as last time. Half-way back across the Channel I saw six 109s approaching but fortunately they were being chased by a Spitfire. I crossed the English coast and looked for an aerodrome but could not find one, but I managed to find a big field. After gliding down to 1,000 ft everything was still under control, but suddenly the cockpit and instruments became covered in thick oil and I could not see what my airspeed was. My speed must have been over 200 mph because I completely overshot the big field, also smaller ones, and my Spitfire went straight through a hedge, leaving its radiator behind, knocked down four trees, at the same time relieved itself of its starboard wing, and then cartwheeled over a pile of felled trees which removed my engine. These little things did not seem to slow the aircraft down. My tail plane had to catch hold of a tree before the fuselage would consider slowing down, but not quickly enough to enable the tail to stay attached to the fuselage.

Once again the rest of the fuselage cartwheeled over a tree and then came to a standstill. For a few seconds I just sat in the remains of my machine and wondered what had happened, but suddenly noticed that the cockpit had caught fire, so I hopped out and ran like hell still with my parachute on and took cover behind the nearest tree. Carefully I looked round the side of the tree. Hell! I could not see a thing out of my right eye. Was I blinded? In a few minutes crowds of people arrived and one person in particular decided that I must have been knocked out and had fallen in the cockpit. He climbed into what was left of the Spitfire, looked in the cockpit and to his dismay could not find anybody. When I dashed up and tapped him on the shoulder he must have thought I was a ghost; because he just stared at me and did not say a word for a few seconds, and after that he only said 'good God!' By now I was fully convinced that I had been blinded, but it was not so; all that had happened was that I had a beautiful black eye.

When I arrived back at my squadron after being in hospital again the blitz was practically over. We only had a few more fights but nothing exciting happened. We as a squadron had shot down over sixty enemy aircraft, another sixty probably, and a good many damaged, for the loss of about seventeen pilots, two of whom were killed accidentally.

The boys are still waiting for the next blitz. A good many of us have had operational experience but these experiences do not affect us like they affect our parents, who worry a lot more than us and I suppose mine will start worrying as soon as I get shot down again. I will now close down as I have been ordered off again to search for a Hun coming in our direction.

NOTE: I did not get him. He ran back home.

*　　*　　*

MATTHEW: we called him Nat – I can't think why; maybe Matthew sounded too biblical and we were blasphemous. Anyway Nat was mad, stark raving mad. He was as thin as a broom-stick, always walked at a jog-trot, had protruding grey eyes and lived right on the end of his nerves. He talked quickly, jerked rather than reacted to situations, never read a book and picked up magazines only to put them down again almost immediately. He had been a champion sprinter at school because his long legs could swoop his light body to the winning post faster than a rat can run away from a bull-terrier. I once pretended to put Nat on a disciplinary charge and he thought I was serious. He was terrified of the consequences. He had landed his Spitfire on the perimeter track for a lark which shows how mad he was. He didn't appreciate the implications. Perimeter tracks are not stressed for a Spitfire dropping on three points with the weight of a full ammunition load, plus fuel and other variations on the theme. Perimeter tracks have on their surface stones, gravel, starter batteries, airmen on bicycles, petrol bowsers. Sometimes there would even be the padre stalking along the track – not that we had our own sky-pilot; but the Parish priests used to come and see us.

Nat was so mad that he once took a padre for a ride in a Spitfire. He sat the parson on his lap – and the Spitfire could hardly contain one man let alone two – and off they went. He couldn't close his cockpit canopy of course, and the padre nearly got his head blown off with the force of the air. Added to which, Nat couldn't use the control column adequately because the padre was sitting on his lap. The Reverend didn't have a parachute strapped on; Nat had forgotten about that. The padre was sick of course because Nat put the Spitfire into a loop. The fact that the Reverend wasn't strapped into the Spitfire never crossed Nat's mind. However, that is not as dangerous as it might seem, because when in a loop the constant gee forces tend to press you down on to the seat and you are not ejected from the cockpit. If Nat had rolled out at the top of the loop, if he had stayed in an inverted position and applied negative gee, the Reverend wouldn't have been alive to conduct his own wake. He would have gone hurtling down to his cemetery, surplice streaming in the wind.

Any observant reader might have noted that Nat's biography is incomplete. This is so because he was killed before he could complete it. I told him he had to write down his recollections and he said he couldn't write and I said so what? When he gave me his half-finished story I told him that he would have to exercise his brain for another few weeks and blow his story up somewhat. The idea bored him but he promised to do it. But the old reaper swung his scythe in Nat's direction and cut his head off quicker than you could say quicksands. Death can come in many ways. Old men go to death; death comes to young men. It all depends on the way the cookie crumbles as George Washington used to say. All that apart, Nat's memory didn't work. His story as he told it is inaccurate; I should know; I was leading him in the air on both occasions when he nearly bought it. I knew more about the subsequent events than Nat. It's impossible to own a decent memory with a brain like Nat's. The front part worked with such speed that the massive unconscious section which comprises three-quarters of the brain was stultified. Memory depends on the massive part not the little bit which controls the impulses, or so I have been informed.

Take his lightship incident. I was given a report on exactly what occurred by Trinity House and the Navy. He belly-landed his Spitfire in the sea, and the radiator slung under the belly together with other configurations immediately caused the aircraft to nose down at a steep angle and he went under the water quicker than a dolphin. He struggled to release his safety harness and in the interim the water changed colour from green to black, meaning he was rather deeper than full fathom five. He shot up to the surface when he kicked himself free. On arrival at the surface he was unconscious, very nearly dead from the weight of water in his lungs. The lightship crew hauled him out just at the moment critique and immediately applied artificial respiration. They only just managed to save his life. When he arrived back on *the squadron he was in a very excitable state; but he was always in an excitable state, he lived on the end of his nerves.*

Next his account of taking down half the trees in East Sussex and surviving the crash is inaccurate. He managed to get two separate incidents confused. Nat was on my wing, I was leading the flight. We were chasing a couple of dozen Messerschmitt pilots heading for France and their French floozies. They were flying flat out at about 25,000 ft and the Spitfire was only about 10 mph faster than the Me 109. It was taking quite a long time for us to catch up and I was studying my fuel gauges with some anxiety. The next thing I knew was that my engine more or less exploded in my face, and so for that matter did Nat's. British ack-ack had, for once, been on target except they hadn't aimed at the Messerschmitts a mile or so ahead of us but at us. So they were on target – the wrong target. I didn't have time to fire my guns at the Messerschmitts before oil covered my windshield and I had to glide back over the white cliffs of Dover where I made a horrible mess of a crash landing and very nearly wrote myself off.

Nat was also hit and had to make a long glide approach over the self-same white cliffs of Dover. He tried to stretch his glide until he was somewhere near East Grinstead. Like he said in his account he was too fast to belly land in the large field he selected. Like he said he couldn't see without sticking his head out of the cockpit because his windshield was covered in oil. Like he said he overshot a couple of other fields before he ran out of air speed and stalled into a woodland.

He certainly removed about forty of the ancient oaks of England when the Spitfire stalled. There was certainly nothing left of his Spitfire except the cockpit and him. He had the devil's luck. What he should have done was what I did. He might have pulled off a better job than I did when I struck terra firma a very heavy blow indeed. He should have hung on to all the altitude possible while he searched for an airfield as near to the coast as he could find. Then he should have spiralled down in the glide, put his airscrew in fine pitch to ease the shock of landing on his belly, orbited the airfield on the descent, taken a hard look at the wind-sock and approached high and fast into the wind. Then he could have virtually dived her into the ground at about ten feet;

then he would have been O.K.; then he wouldn't have written off forty of England's ancient oaks and darned nearly killed himself.

Nat began to run out of steam in the Spring of 1941 mainly because he kept finishing up in hospital and was extremely attracted by the nurses and they kept putting up his pulse-rate. So he was removed from operations and sent to be an instructor at a fighter operational conversion unit. Shortly afterwards, one of his pupils flying in a training Spitfire collided with him and cut Nat's tail off, and they both finished up thirty feet down under the Gloucestershire sod. I tried to shoot myself when I received the information but, fortunately, or unfortunately, my .38 Colt wasn't loaded.

The kiss of death, I suppose.

CHAPTER FIVE

PETER

VIVIDLY do I remember my first encounter with the Hun. I had been in the squadron about a month and was lucky to gain valuable operational experience after such a short time; we were in a quiet area based on East Anglia. The encounter took place some eighty miles out to sea (I still shudder at the thought) and I attacked as No. 2 of my section. It was a Junker 88 and I recall how, instead of concentrating on the enemy as I thought I would do, I was more concerned with my instrument-panel; that was before I got within range, of course. I had expected to be alarmed by the fire of the rear gunner, but to my surprise I was totally unmoved by it. As soon as I was within firing range I let him have it, aiming at the aeroplane in general instead of concentrating on the engines, as I would now do. I killed the rear gunner and when I left him – the other two of the section finished their attacks before I did – the Ju 88 was pouring glycol from one engine. It struck me on the run home that not once had I noticed a swastika or even absorbed details of the aircraft; the thing had somehow seemed ominous and un-British. Recognition had not been necessary. Straining my eyes for that welcome glimpse of land, and checking my compass with the sun, I returned to England, home and beauty, feeling quite a dog and a goer despite the fact that my score was but one-third of a damaged Ju 88. The experience gained, however, proved extremely valuable in the future.

After this encounter there was a lull for a week, during which we spent our flying time in practise dog-fights – both a spectacular and useful pastime – mock attacks and interceptions, displays for various spectators, beating up the home of the inevitable girl-friend at low level, and innumerable unsuccessful interception patrols. On one occasion I was having a practise dogfight with Billy. I was both inexperienced and not too fit at the time as I had a heavy cold and one of my evasive tactics was a roll off the top of a loop. I hung on top for a bit upside down and the petrol in the exhaust manifolds burned solidly for about ten seconds – it seemed like ten hours. I thought that Billy had given me a squirt and that I was on fire. On landing my face was the colour of green cheese and Billy (then my Flight-Commander) made me accompany him on a four-mile run that evening in order to get me in trim. Dear old Billy. He's dead now, of course.

Another of our more serious if boring tasks was to perform convoy patrols and many an hour did I spend flying backwards and forwards over convoys, wondering what it was like to be sailing the seas with aircraft droning overhead. I was particularly interested in thinking of how the sailors viewed us airmen – whether they thought we were a set of over-publicized young scatterbrains or whether they bore the same admiration for us as we did for them, the men who strove against storm and tempest, submarines and enemy bombs.

Gradually the war in the air began to escalate; things down south got hotter; more and more enemy aircraft were shot down; we began to flap more often; monthly flying hours increased. The boys began to shoot down and chase more Huns, we shot down six on six successive days. Then came my second encounter with the enemy. A Dornier 17 was spotted at 27,000 ft by Nat, who was No. 3 in the section. We gave chase and caught him about forty miles out to sea at 10,000 ft. I closed to attack and my No. 2 came up abreast of me to distract the rear gunners. We fired simultaneously, broke, and attacked again. He was obviously hit. Nat then attacked and I watched him. He came up like a bat out of hell and broke sharply nearly colliding with the stricken Hun, smoke pouring from his eight Brownings. Return fire stopped, we went in again and Jerry turned for England – the sign of surrender. We followed closely, watching for any signs of a trap. Smoke poured from his engines; he was in a bad way. Suddenly his nose dropped and he dived almost vertically. A most impressive sight it was, the big twin-engined aircraft hurtling earthwards with great streams of smoke following it. Down, down, down – would he never pull out I wondered? He didn't. With the most terrific splash I'd ever seen he hit the sea and disintegrated. I circled the spot but could see nothing but oil. I was jubilant; my second engagement and successful; life was very full. I flew back to base at zero feet and cut some capers over a lightship on the way. But Nat was reported missing after this encounter.

A few days later we had some momentous news. We were ordered to go down south where the big air blitz of 1940 was just beginning. Within twelve hours we had packed our bags and moved off. I remember wondering as we flew over our old base in a squadron beat-up, how many of our pilots would be alive to tell the tale next month. On landing at our new base we were ordered off almost immediately on patrol, from which we all returned without seeing anything. I landed feeling rather disgruntled and thinking that all the tales of mass attacks were so much rot; I was soon to be disillusioned.

Next morning we went off at dawn to an advanced base and after a hasty breakfast there we were ordered to scramble. Off we went. I felt a little frightened. At 20,000 ft over Dover we suddenly sighted about 300 German aircraft returning to France from the direction of London. Aha, I thought! Here it comes. Buster squadron headed for the formations, which were being attacked by other British fighters. We burst into the middle of the German fighters and bombers and I singled out a formation of four Heinkels below me.

Down I went at about 450 mph and after pulling up I squirted the bomber on the port side of the formation with my guns. Black smoke oozed from his port engine. I came down again, squirted the whole formation and then spotted four or five Me 109s in my mirror. I thought: plenty of time, pal, fifty per cent of people are bumped off in their first big scrap. So down went the old nose and at about 500 mph I screeched earthwards.

The Intelligence Officer was waiting for me as I landed and I told him I had damaged a Heinkel, then he interviewed the next pilot. Everyone was bubbling over with excitement, each man had fired at something and several were able to claim certainties. Two of the boys had baled-out and had thus become members of the famous Caterpillar Club.

It was a successful start to our sojourn down south, for we had bagged five certainties and three probables with other German aircraft damaged. From then on life became a series of hastily-eaten meals which were often missed altogether; patrols at all hours of the day and binges in the evenings when we were not so dog-tired that we had to go to bed early.

On my second patrol in the front-line I had a narrow escape which warned me of the danger of being caught napping. We had engaged a large number of German fighters and all I could see was a mass of aircraft milling round in every conceivable attitude. Suddenly I saw a Me 109 just below me and in my ignorance flew straight at him, shooting as I went. The next thing I knew was that something hit me from behind, that my guns had stopped firing and that I was spinning down. One glance in my mirror gave me the information that two or three Me 109s were coming after me. I came out of the spin and continued in a near vertical attitude at something over 500 mph. I pulled out at about 5,000 ft and then found that one of my ailerons did not work and that all my electrical gear was unserviceable. Hurriedly pinpointing my position I headed for base, keeping a wary eye open for force-landing fields as I did so. On reaching my base I approached to land, and while holding off my wing suddenly dropped. I thought that I was going to spin in, but fortunately I kept her going. It was due to the disturbance of the aileron balance. As I taxied in I saw another Spitfire land with one aileron shot right off by a cannon shell. On examination I found that two of my aileron wires were completely shot away, my radio set was punctured and there were seven bullet holes in the fuselage directly behind my armour plate. Phew!

The next day we went up as usual and mixed it with large numbers of Me 109s. I had not been able to get a bead on anything and was manoeuvring to get my sights on a Hun when I saw an aircraft getting into position behind me. I adopted violent evasive action and came out just behind it, when I saw that it was a Spitfire which then sheared off. Whether or not the pilot would have taken a short squirt at me I do not know, for one fighter looks very much like another from astern and in a mêlée. I did not have any success that day, but when on my way back to my base at about 1,000 ft I saw an aeroplane falling at a colossal speed from the sky. When at about 500 ft it flicked on to its back and hit the earth at something like 600 mph. There was a violent explosion and a sheet of flame was all that remained. High above I saw a parachute floating idly down. Lucky for him he was not in that plane.

The next patrol brought more fortune in its train, for we saw a big He 111 bomber separated from its squadron attempting to make an unobtrusive getaway to France. Two of us left the squadron to deal with this intruder and after a few squirts I could see that the propellers had stopped ticking over. He then made a crash-landing in a wood clearing, and the other pilot and I saw three of the crew get out – the fourth was dead I suppose. While these Germans clustered round the wreck of their Heinkel we circled the spot until we saw army troops arrive and they took them prisoner. As soon as they were in safe hands I dived straight at them and did an upward Charlie over them – not good for the engine but I thought it excusable. The fact that only three men got out set me pondering on the subject of air gunners. The courage of a man who can stay at his post with such machines as Spitfires and Hurricanes, or for that matter even Me 109s, attacking him is difficult to comprehend. Horrid tales are often told about dead rear gunners being scraped into jampots and the like. For my part I had nothing but admiration for them.

Despite the hardships, however, the several weeks when the blitz was in full swing will rank as some of the happiest of my life. The spirit of the squadron under the moral uplift of such a personality as our then Squadron Commander was extremely high. Life was cheap and the general atmosphere was devil-may-care; some of the scenes in our mess were indescribable. How can one do justice on paper to such scenes as when our Intelligence Officer fell downstairs clad only in a bath-towel and a tin hat when the sirens sung the immediate danger message. Or how Nat pinched the kitty of our poker school when we were ordered off one day, and went chasing out to his aeroplane yelling that he was going to get himself shot down so that we would lose our money.

Then we were ordered to move to a new base and amid much cursing the stores and transport left by road. The squadron flew to our new base, which we found immensely to our liking, as there was a noticeable lack of formality around the place. After the scramble for decent bedrooms had subsided, we celebrated that night by having a colossal binge. After taking down the Intelligence Officer's trousers and washing his belly with beer, we decided to go to bed, well pleased with our day's work.

Dawn broke next day to find us at readiness with a special mission to perform. Three of us volunteered to protect a twin-engine reconnaissance aircraft which was spotting for the long-range guns based at Dover. Off we went and patrolled Calais while all the flak in Germany appeared to open upon us. We were there for an hour before the spotter turned for home, and like so many sheep-dogs guarding their flock we took it home. A very interesting experience it was too, if rather prolonged in terms of nervous strain.

The next few days passed peacefully enough, the only incidents of note being when we found several German bombers limping home over the coast. We finished them off without any opposition. It proved to be, however, just the calm before the storm.

September 7, 1940, dawned clear and bright. We were out of bed before first light and everything appeared to be as it always was. We were ordered up on patrol just as I was playing chess with Mac. 'Hang on, Mac' I said, 'I'll be back with you in an hour or two!' And off we went. No sooner had we got to combat altitude than we saw a formation of bombers and fighters just above us. 'O.K., boys,' the C.O. said over the R/T, 'We're going into the attack.' Getting under the formation we all climbed right into the middle. I was number two to the squadron-commander and followed him up. I was just about stalled when we were in the middle so I levelled out, and let the formation pass me by head on while I fired my guns. You could almost see the look of surprise on the faces of those Dorniers. At one moment they were sailing along in tight formation *en route* for London, and the next minute twelve Spitfires simply grew among them. They broke up in every angle and attitude imaginable. After our initial attack there were thirty odd hapless Dorniers all over the sky with no chance in the world of survival.

After making a head-on attack on a bomber I hauled round at about four gee and came round on his tail. After a squirt or two, one of his engines blew up which splashed oil and glycol all over my windscreen; the other engine started to burn. I waved good-bye and looked for more. I saw a He 111 making for cloud below me, so I went down in a dive, opened fire at extreme range and broke at the last possible moment. I thought I'd collide with him because my controls were so stiff at the speed I was travelling I could hardly manoeuvre the Spitfire. I only just scraped him in fact. I climbed above him and watched. His whole tail unit was on fire and his engines were smoking. I came down for another squirt just before he went into cloud, and whilst I was squirting he vanished from sight and was seen no more (I hope). On landing I found that we had got rid of twelve for certain with many more probables. But I was extremely annoyed because that twerp of an Intelligence Officer only gave me one certain of my two. My feelings were partly mollified on finding that Fighter Command as a whole had claimed 185 Jerry planes destroyed that day. Maybe my certainty-which-was-only-a-probable was not so important after all.

The next few days were quieter, but soon we had another good day. We suddenly intercepted some Me 109s over the coast and I protected Mac's tail while he got busy doing one in. It blew up after two short squirts, then we got together and went after four more aircraft. 'It's O.K., pal,' I called to Mac on the R/T. 'They're friendly, I think.' 'Maybe you're right,' he replied, 'but we'll just make sure.' Then he said 'Christ, they're 109s!' Up we went. I took on two, Mac took on the other two. I squirted one and he went for home. Fastening on to the tail of the other, I gave him a good one. His nose went down vertically. I followed. Down we screeched at about 400 mph. We passed the coast, I squirted again, keeping a wary eye open for his boy friend. Suddenly his speed dropped and I saw a stream of glycol. 'You poor blighter' I thought. Then I gave him a long one. Pieces fell off. He faltered, then hit the sea and vanished. I looked around but saw nothing, and so returned at zero feet feeling a prize shocker.

The next engagement we had was against the much-vaunted Messerschmitt 110. We saw the formation being chased by some Hurricanes. Being decent types, we nipped in to help. I'd never seen a 110 before, they had two engines and I thought for a moment that they were bombers. Consequently I made a head-on attack at them. I soon realized my folly because their forward-firing armament was formidable. I was doing nearly 400 mph and they were nigh on 300 mph and we were passing each other at about 700 mph, which is pretty fast. I fired all the time, but saw no results. By the time I had turned to follow them they were miles away. I flew at maximum speed but could only catch up with a straggler which was being attacked by a couple of Hurricanes. It was their meat, so I left them to it. I particularly noticed that the 110s would fly straight for a short while, and then form a defensive circle, thus making somewhat erratic progress home. I learned later that of the twenty or more Me 110s that came over, about fifteen were shot down.

As I was returning to my base, I saw a Hurricane ahead of me, and decided to test the pilot's reactions. I made a mock attack on him, but before I got into range he had whirled round in a tight Immelmann. I flew alongside and stuck up a couple of fingers, to which he grinningly replied. He certainly had all his wits about him.

At dawn next day operations asked for a pilot to make a weather reconnaissance of the Channel, so off I went. I snooped around about mid-Channel but the fish weren't biting, so I had to return somewhat despondent.

We were sent off the following day as per usual – Jerry had not yet got fed up with us – and whilst patrolling I saw a 109 in the distance. I had lagged behind the squadron, having been delayed on the take-off by a rigger – not my usual one – who had forgotten to switch on my main oxygen supply, so I didn't bother to tell any one, but slipped off unobserved. I appeared to catch him napping because I got right under him before I fired. Then I gave him three seconds of hot lead right in the guts. The aircraft gave a distinct shudder, the pilot must have turned to see who I was, but then continued on his way. I noticed the tell-tale stream of glycol, but closed for another bang. Full and square I hit him, and saw his tail struts fall off, and a large piece of fuselage, probably his hood, came off. He went down just on top of a cloud layer, and carried on. Swearing under my breath, I caught him up, got right up to him and gave him the full works. Black smoke oozed, and he fell through the cloud. I followed, and found myself north of Dungeness. But could I see that benighted Jerry? Could I hell? I circled the spot for a quarter of an hour, looking,

looking, looking. I was then at 4,000 ft and a 109 with most of its guts shot away could not have gone far before it fell into the sea. I returned in a flaming temper, and told the I.O. where the Messerschmitt fell. He was unable to confirm this as a kill and so I was only given a probable. Probable my foot! If that Jerry got so much as half-way across the Channel I'd eat my longerons. When I thought about it later, I realized I had almost certainly killed the pilot on my second attack, and the aircraft was flying itself.

That night we had an all-squadron binge in the nearby town. Nat had three half-pints of bitter, and changed from a nervous, quiet schoolboy into a lusty, noisy, excitable young man. It is no exaggeration to say that he has never been the same man since – an amazing phenomenon. We arrived back in the small hours, threw furniture at each other and then went to bed.

There was a bit of a lull after this. Jerry had changed his tactics from large numbers of bombers and small fighter escorts, and then few bombers and many fighters, and was now on the all-fighter stage where their value was merely nuisance. They always flew very high, and would come in and drop a few bombs and then go back again. This didn't give us a lot of time for interception purposes, but we often had a crack at them.

We were chasing some who were a bit higher than we were one day, and we all got split up. I was after one bloke at over 32,000 ft over the Channel, and was slowly gaining range on him. By the time I got within range we were over France, and so I lost no time, but gave one short burst and then a very long one from about 400 yards. I had obviously hit him, and he turned over and went down vertically in a cloud of white smoke. He may have landed safely, baled out, or gone straight into the deck, so I could only claim a damaged for that. I returned towards England, when suddenly my windscreen was covered with oil. Hastily checking my instruments, I saw my oil pressure registering zero and the glycol and oil temperatures rising. I switched off the engine and prepared to force-land. I had plenty of height, but a long way to go, so I headed for the nearest part of the coast. I crossed at about 3,000 ft, and just made an aerodrome. I had no height in which to turn into wind, and so I had to land down-wind. I came over the boundary fast – always better to overshoot than undershoot – and held off. She floated for hundreds of yards with the wind, and when she touched down it was obvious that I was going into the boundary hedge. I had my brakes full on, but the grass was wet.

Just as the hedge loomed up, I put my hand on my gun-sight to protect my head. That was the last thing I remembered for a little while, and when I came to, my first instinct was to get out of the aeroplane. I had no idea where I was, or how I came to be there. A night in bed was enough though, and I returned to my station next day by road, and went home for a few days' sick leave.

When I got back after my sick leave, I found that the weather had been too bad for much flying, so I didn't miss much. After I had once again settled down we had another considerable dog-fight with a bunch of Messerschmitts. I had a hangover from a cold at the time and was not really fighting fit. The 109s had formed a defensive circle at about 30,000 ft, and we were endeavouring to break it up. Eventually they split up all over the sky, and I lost sight of them. I dived and was tooling round at about 15,000 ft, the height to which I imagined they had gone, and, incidentally, was keeping a wary eye in at least three dimensions, when I suddenly heard a rattle of gun-fire. I swung instinctively, and a 109 with a huge red nose flashed past me, levelled out, and then did a complete flick roll before going earthwards. I was so surprised that I didn't get a bead on him. I followed him down vowing vengeance, gave him a few squirts at close range and at about 2,000 ft we crossed over Dungeness, heading out to sea. Then a 109, followed by a Spitfire, flashed across my bows, in a manner of speaking, and momentarily distracted my attention. I searched the sky but my 109 had disappeared. I looked everywhere, but could not find him. To this day I feel sure he went straight into the sea, but as I didn't see him crash to his death I could claim nothing. I swore in three different languages and climbed to look for more trouble. I found it in the shape of another Hun coming towards me. I gave him a quickee head-on and then he disappeared. I turned hard around and saw another Spitfire come down on him, smoke pouring from its guns. The German was a dead duck.

Then came the lull. Nothing happened for weeks. The

newspapers began to gloat over our victories and we got fed-up because we couldn't repeat them. Reaction set in, and we went haywire. I remember one night when we came home in a convoy of three shooting-brakes with toilet paper streaming out of the windows. Every car we passed would get some toilet paper, and many were the verbal exchanges we had with innocent motorists. One night we had a terrific beat-up in the mess, a requisitioned country mansion. Busts were blackleaded to look like Hitler, much cock-fighting and wrestling took place. We blacked Mac's face so he looked like a nigger boy. We dressed up in the most sensational clothes and finished the night by being hounded up and down corridors and around the house and grounds by Mac with a .38 Colt in his hand. He was drunk out of his mind and the Colt was loaded!

Soon after this we moved to a new base where we settled down to station routine, after a long spell at single-squadron bases. We had been there about a fortnight but we had seen no action and were pretty browned off. Then came that glorious day. We intercepted about 40 Ju 87s, accompanied by some escorting fighters, just before they reached their target, a coastal town. I was one of a section dispatched to intercept a single raider when we spotted them. I rubbed my eyes when I saw these lumbering dive-bombers; I couldn't believe that it could be true. Then, with a howl of delight, I went straight into the middle. I spent the next few minutes attacking and breaking up innumerable formations of these dive-bombers. I saw two break sharply and jettison their bombs, obviously hit. Then I made a longer attack on another which heeled over with oil pouring from the engine. I had no time to follow him down as I was too busy transferring my attack to another. My technique was to go straight for the sections of German aircraft from every imaginable angle until they split up their formations. It was an impressive sight as we battled over the target. I could see some of the 87s go down vertically on to the target, and drop their bombs to the accompaniment of ack-ack of every calibre. Huge columns of water rose as the bombs exploded, and flashes and shell-bursts could be seen everywhere. In the general mêlée I saw Spitfires attacking from all angles with their guns smoking as they fired. One pilot fired as he was on his back – or maybe I was on my back – I couldn't tell.

Aircraft distintegrated around me. I saw them catch fire, go straight down, smoking, into the sea. It was vivid. Dante would have gone into ecstasies if he could have changed places with me. Satan would have found the atmosphere quite homelike. It was the acme of aerial combat. Flame, smoke, gunpowder, death, and hell, all mixed up; undoubtedly the finest moment of my life.

The formations had been split up. Individual dive-bombers were left, all vulnerable to attack. Enough I thought; now for the kill. The next 87 I saw I chased after and watched his bomb drop harmlessly into the sea. Then came the attack. Tracer bullets, cannon shells, explosive shells, every type of ground defence was in action. They were firing at my chosen target, but I was close behind and got the benefit of quite a lot. My Junkers was at last out of range of ground defences, and I could now get down to business. I wiped the ice off my wind-screen and made a quarter attack on him. I closed right up to him before he broke, but there was no fire from the rear gunner. I realized by this time that my ammunition must be getting short, and that I had better finish him off before it ran out. I closed to point-blank range, accordingly, and fired deliberately, taking careful aim. I saw my explosive ammunition hit its mark. A thin tongue of flame crept from the port side of his engine. I climbed above him and watched the flame gradually spread; it welled up until it surrounded the cockpit. The nose of the Junkers gradually fell, and then he went right into the sea. He hit the water with a huge splash, and vanished. Only oil was left. I circled the spot, saw nothing of the debris and then returned home, taking note of a few holes in my wings as I went. When I landed I found that one of my ailerons was held by only two strands of wire, and, incidentally, that at least seventeen of the raiders had perished.

The next incident of any note that occurred was when we went up on an interception patrol in rather poor weather. We did not see any Jerries, and on our return found that the weather had deteriorated very badly, and that there was thick fog over Southern England. We were trying to find our base, and time was passing, till eventually I was flying with my eyes on my petrol gauge nearly the whole time. By the grace of God we just made an aerodrome and as I landed I heard voices on the radio. As each pilot landed he expressed his relief by blasphemy, foul cursing, and any other thing that came into his strained mind. It was rather amusing to listen to as one sat on good old Mother Earth, but it might have proved a disastrous trip. We had a terrific party that night and we slept on the floor of a friend's house.

A few days later we took off on another patrol, and just as we had gained our necessary height I suddenly lost control of my aircraft and the nose of another Spitfire materialized vertically in front of me. My airscrew was knocked off and my lateral controls were non-effective. I opened up my hood, most of which was knocked off anyway, parts missing my head by inches, and contemplated the situation.

My aircraft was obviously severely damaged: I might possibly make a forced landing but this was unlikely as there was a ground mist and I would not be able to see hills, trees, and things like that until I hit them. Further, my much weakened airframe might be in the process of distintegration for all I knew. Accordingly, I undid my straps, looked at the altimeter which showed 5,000 ft, and let the airflow pull me out of the cockpit with my hand on the rip-cord of the parachute. Next thing I knew was that I was floating earthwards with a huge silk canopy over my head. I gasped with relief, for my decision had of necessity been hurried and I had not considered the possibility of my parachute not opening.

On reaching the ground I hung up a thirty-foot tree for some time in the middle of a wood, whilst I could hear the Army, Home Guard, and sundry others crashing through the undergrowth towards me. I detached myself from the parachute and swarmed down the tree. On reaching the ground I was greeted by two small boys who had magically appeared before the authorities had. One of them said to me, 'How are you mister?' to which I managed to reply, 'Fine, thank you.' Then came the Army, rifles in hand, followed by the Home Guard, and finally an old farmer, shot-gun pointed at my head, his devout spouse clinging to his trousers, apparently trying to hold him back. I took a quick swig of brandy from my flask, and then felt equal, at the worst, to a charge of buckshot in my nether regions.

I managed to shake off the authorities, and found a good type of Army officer with a couple of buxom wenches, who took me to their delightful home, and there ladled up the largest whisky and spot of soda I had ever seen. The police were kicking up a bit of a shindig outside; jealous, I expect, so I bid my charming hostesses adieu and departed back to my squadron via the police station and an Army car.

I went up as usual next day, but for the first quarter of an hour felt distinctly uneasy. There followed a lull of a few days and then a large stroke of luck when my section was ordered to intercept a single raider, whilst we were on patrol. Within five minutes of receiving the order I had spotted him. He saw me too, for he turned hot-foot for home. No use, however, for my Spitfire was faster than his 109. I caught him up, and after two very short bursts the Messerschmitt caught fire and the pilot baled-out. I only used twenty rounds from each gun on him, which represents a half-second burst. That ended for me the Blitz of 1940.

* * *

PETER was my best friend. I'm not homosexually inclined but I was in love with Peter, platonically in love. We lived in this fighter squadron, Buster Squadron, and that's exactly like living in a monastery – believe it or not. So Peter was my monkish brother and in a kind of manner we took Holy Communion together. I even went so far as to administer the last rites to him, in a manner of speaking. Peter's manner of dying was quite shocking, quite obscene. I will never forget it. I think I will always want to remember it; Heaven knows why, I certainly don't.

He was a tall chap, lugubrious on the face of it; in fact he possessed a great sense of rather dry humour. He was the son of an old man; you can always identify the sons of old men because they look like old men, with lined, wrinkled faces and Peter was barely twenty-one years of age.

Peter was comparatively rich, certainly richer than I was. He was a bit of a poseur, a bit of a spoilt boy; an only son, quite well educated at a school based between Windsor and Slough called Eton College. Mine was self-education; for everyone it's self-education in fact but only the self-educated appreciate this; you've got to learn the hard way. The University of Life is the only decent academy for advanced studies in the world.

Peter certainly had guts, he certainly enjoyed getting engaged with the Hun. This is not to suggest that he was not fearful; I am sure he said his prayers when his Spitfire rolled off the line. Peter would have made a first-class Prime Minister. He had sufficient intellect for the job, he was as cynical as the Rt. Hon. Harold Macmillan and he had presence. How does one define presence? It is quite impossible so I will barely make the attempt. All I say is that the room lit up without the need for electricity when Peter entered it. That's presence. Peter was an above average fighter pilot, but somehow it seemed out of character; he was too gentle for a start. Furthermore I would have thought that fighter pilots, natural fighter pilots like me, should be short and I am only 5 ft 8in. If you were much over six feet in height you couldn't sit in a Spitfire in any case. Even if the seat in the cockpit was lowered to its bottom rung you couldn't close the canopy if you were six foot three.

Peter didn't bite his finger-nails. Most good fighter pilots ate their finger ends. His nails were well manicured. I could never understand it. On the ground Peter appeared to be a languorous sort of chap, easy-going, slow of reaction, a natural gentleman. In fact, when in the air in his Spitfire, he was fast as an electric eel. His reactions were decidedly over-sharp. I jumped him one day just for fun, just to test his reactions. He saw me coming, he didn't know whether I was a Messerschmitt or a Spitfire or a Hurricane. It was extremely stupid of me. He waited until I was almost within firing range, hauled back in a steep turn at four and a half gee and was on my tail before you could say Jack Robinson. Thank God his aircraft recognition was good, else he would have blown me up. All he did in the event was to catch up and fly in close formation with me. Then he very delicately put up two fingers of his gauntleted hands. But he knew he had me cold and I am supposed to be a fighter ace. Which must mean that granted luck Peter would have finished up as an accredited ace and then got a cushy job looking after the King or somebody. But he didn't have luck. Or to put it another way: they say there's a divinity in odd numbers, either in nativity, chance or death. And, let it be noted, Peter was twenty-one years of age when he bought it. Or in other words he creased himself when he was an odd number. However that may or may not be, Peter was an odd chap. Wherein I speak of disastrous chances, moving accidents, hairbreadth escapes and all that sort of thing.

But Peter's manner of dying was rather unusual. Buster Squadron was at fifteen minutes readiness and we were playing games of cards or chess or things like that. We were based on a grass airfield which meant we were, for reasons too complicated to explain, fast reactors to the scramble order. As was normal, Dorothy Lamour was singing about desert islands via a gramophone record over the Tannoy microphone which was contained in the pilots' dispersal hut. I conjured up mental images of Miss Lamour and she was good, very good. She made me feel like I needed a woman not the scramble order. I didn't want to join the Air Force, I didn't want to go to war; I just wanted to hang around Piccadilly underground, living on the earnings of a high-born lady.

Then the sector controller rang up on the field telephone and ordered us to come up to two minutes readiness. I hated sector controllers and I still hate telephones. They always invited you to come to more or less immediate readiness. All we did was to pull on our flying overalls as our parachutes, helmets, gauntlets and other accoutrements were, in any case, already stacked in piles by our Spitfires. Then we went on playing cards or what have you.

Then the field telephone rang again, the airman manning it almost immediately began to wave his hand violently, meaning it was the scramble order and everyone started to move towards the door of the hut. Some chap grabbed the microphone and bawled over the Tannoy 'Buster Squadron scramble, interception vector 130 degrees, bandits approaching at angels thirty.' This I vaguely heard as I jog-trotted to my Spitfire, where my rigger helped me to get the parachute strapped on and the engine fitter assisted me with the safety harness once I was in the cockpit. We taxied out in wide echelon and the squadron commander waited twenty seconds to allow the late starters to get into position and then he busted his throttle wide open and climbed on a vector of 130 degrees. We went up with him and climbed to 30,000 ft where we saw nothing.

Then I observed Peter's Spitfire begin to bank over, almost imperceptibly, away from the squadron formation. I watched as he heeled over further and began to go into a dive. I broke formation and followed him, and his dive became almost a vertical dive. I put the nose down even *further and went after him. I tried to work out what went wrong. I thought the only cause must be anoxia, that his oxygen tube had slipped out of its socket as he turned his neck. I reckon I was plumb right in my prognosis. He was still at full throttle and my speed soon began to exceed the design limitations of the Spitfire as calculated by R. J. Mitchell. He had been flying as Green One; I was Blue One. I started to bawl over the R/T in terms of 'Green One for Christ's sake pull out!' I then said 'Peter, for God's sake pull out!'*

He didn't hear me. He must have been in a state of anoxia. He was diving too fast to be able to come to his senses in time. I realized this. I didn't know what the hell to do about it. All I could do was to pull out of my dive at the last possible moment before I struck terra firma. Then I watched his Spitfire explode on contact with the ground and solemnly flew around estimating the size of the hole in the ground he had made. It was a crater of about twenty feet from end to end and it probably went down thirty feet. He hit the earth at something between 500 and 600 mph. On landing back at base, the riggers discovered that the fuselage of my Spitfire was distorted. I had indeed exceeded the design limitations of the Spitfire.

Peter had gone to Hell before the Devil had time to arrange the reception committee.

CHAPTER SIX

SERGEANT-PILOT BIDMEAN

*SERGEANT-PILOT BIDMEAN had no tale to tell, so I
had better tell it for him. He arrived on Buster Squadron in
late September 1940, when the heat was still on although
Kesselring had stopped flying his balbos by day; because the
Luftwaffe then commenced their fighter bomber phase. Not
that General Sperile had also stopped his Luftwaffe
bombers operating by night, by no means had he done that.
Bidmean was appointed to my flight, and I had him come in
with his pilot's flying log-book to the tent which formed my
office. The squadron-commander had no time to interview
him personally, so he threw the baby at me. I didn't blame
him for this. He almost invariably led Buster Squadron
whereas I managed to duck a few sorties now and again. We
were by no means martinets in disciplinary terms in 1940.
We wore flying overalls most of the time so there were no
uniform buttons which needed polishing, or any of that kind
of thing. Nevertheless, there was a certain standard to which
everyone had to conform; all a matter of self-discipline in
fact; which is the best form of discipline. Bidmean turned up
for his first formal interview with filthy buttons on his tunic
and a smirk on his face. The smirk was easy enough to wipe
off but I wasn't going to clean his buttons for him. The
average virtuous chap takes care of his appearance ahead of
his first formal interview; Bidmean didn't. Then he had his
cap set on one side of his head just as if he were Admiral
Beatty's grandson. He wore kid gloves intended for the use of
officers not NCOs. I knew, within five seconds that he was
yellow, that he was lacking in moral fibre, but you've got to
assume that errors of judgement can occasionally occur. So I
sat him down in the only available chair in the tent, whereupon he crossed his legs like he was in his granny's parlour.*

His salute had been sloppy as they come; but he had, at least, remembered to salute. He then tried to con me. As a matter of fact I then conned him. I pretended he interested me very much and he tried to rouse my temper so I would kick him off Buster Squadron without further ado and send him to a target-towing flight where he wouldn't be shot at by the Luftwaffe. It was all very interesting.

I made the pretence of inspecting his flying log-book with great care although there was, of course, no need for me to do that. I already knew all about it. He had flown a hundred and fifty pilot hours, about forty of those with his flying training instructor in the other seat. He had flown the Tiger Moth, a Miles Magister, a North American Harvard, and a Spitfire while at his operational training unit. He was raw as a barrel-load of green potatoes and he was yellow as a chick. He was a verbose little cockney playing the extrovert when he was introverted out of his wits. He was hoping like hell I would kick him off the squadron soonest. Then he could retain his pilot's brevet, fly on non-operational duties and impress his personality on the locals in his pub as a warrior. He must have been as callow as they come and he was a most unpleasant little man aged about twenty – the same age as me.

I continued my conmanship and explained that I was asking ten pilots in Buster Squadron to write about their experiences because I had the nous to appreciate that this might turn out to be valuable historical data. I said to Bidmean that I would be honoured if he would put his thoughts and experiences down on paper when he had gained enough experience in combat conditions. He smirked and said he would do that. I knew he couldn't write but that was relatively unimportant. Few of the other pilots in this book could write anyway, that's why their accounts are so interesting – or so I find them.

Bidmean left my tent and I sat behind my desk and brooded. He did what I thought he would do. He went straight to sick-quarters, explained to the medico that he had just joined the squadron but he felt ill. The Medical Officer must have been in need of psychiatric assistance on his own account because he left Bidmean alone with the thermometer stuck in his mouth. I have no doubt that Bidmean then took it out and lit a match under it and then wiped off

88

the evidence. The M.O. noted that he had a temperature of 102 degrees and sent him off home on a week's sick-leave. Whereupon Bidmean conned his local doctor and managed to stay away from Buster Squadron for another fortnight.

The Luftwaffe were still busy making use of fighter sweeps which put us at a tactical disadvantage; and they escalated the policy by flying fighter bomber attacks indiscriminately on London. By now, the Me 109s were fitted with two 20 mm cannon and two machine-guns whereas we only had the light batteries of eight 0.303 in machine-guns. They heavily out-gunned us but we had more guts than they did. In any case, we were protecting British air space and they had no right to enter it. So we used to get pretty angry. They normally had the advantage of height, of the sun, of their high cruising speeds and of the tactical initiative. There was not a lot to choose between the Spitfire and Me 109. They could fly higher than we could, but we had a speed advantage of about 10 mph and the Spitfire was more manoeuvrable than the Messerschmitt. We were faster on the dive, provided we could overcome the initial handicap of our carburettors not reacting kindly to negative gee conditions, whereas the Daimler Benz engines of the Me 109 with direct fuel injection most certainly gave them an important advantage. Finally, as they could select their moment to penetrate British air space, they could also make sure the sun was on their side; King Sol was our worst enemy, King Sol in 1940 was so to say a naturalized German.

All these, it might be thought, are boring and technical details. They are in fact life and death messages; they certainly were to us. So, while my colleagues and I were enduring on an average of four times a day encounters with the jagdgeschwaders of the fighter arm of the Luftwaffe, Bidmean spent three happy weeks emanating line-shoots in his local pub as to how many Huns he had actually shot down. He was, after all, formally entitled to wear the flying brevet or pilots' wings of the RAF because he had passed his flying tests and arrived at that stage of training. We all had to wear uniform dress in those days in any case. I have no doubt that he impressed his girl-friends with his glamour as a fighter pilot, because he was on the nominal roll, even though he had only formed up in front of me in Buster Squadron and had then immediately faked his way into being granted sick-leave.

In the course of time he reluctantly returned to Buster Squadron and I pretended to be as sympathetic as I had previously been. I told him we could not afford to send him off on a training sortie because Spitfires were still in short supply, so he would have to learn the vital navigational pin-points from maps. I set up on my desk a map which showed Kent, East Sussex and other Home Counties and drew lines and circles around the essential navigational pin-points — like the railway which runs direct from east to west and vice versa from somewhere like Margate to Woking. Then I told him he would be detailed for the first operational sortie next morning which meant he would have to get out of his bed at about four a.m., wait for first light and wait for dawn to catch up with first light. Then he would have to twitch like I did until the scramble order arrived over the field telephone. When he was in the air with the squadron, I lied, he would feel happy as a sand-boy, all his nerve-ends would stop hammering and so on.

Dawn hit the sky the next morning like a volcano erupting. It also hit the fighter controller at the sector operations room when someone woke him up and reported fifty plus bandits on their way to Margate. He was not a very good controller, in fact, but he did have the authority to order us into the air and we normally obliged, so when he gave us the scramble order we took off. Bidmean, somehow or other, managed to attach himself alongside my starboard wing-tip as instructed while I was on the climb. I watched him like a hawk every second I could spare. I was leading Buster Squadron as the squadron commander, Crispin, had a heavy cold and had prudently decided for once to stay on the ground. In due course the controller informed me that there was a jagdgeschwader of Messerschmitts at 35,000 ft proceeding inland at something over 300 mph. He estimated there were fifty in the formation. I decided to climb on a southerly heading over the Channel; try and get above them and jump them out of the sun when they turned for home. So I continued in my climb.

'Buster leader. Bandits 12 o'clock high, smoking.' It was Raymond's voice.

'Understood' I replied. I peered into the azure blue of the

sky and saw them. They were high above leaving contrails only 100 yards long. 'I see them' I then replied over the R/T.

I had deliberately made Bidmean my number two, flying on my right wing. His job was to guard my tail. Slight hope of that but better than detailing him to protect another section leader. When I next looked out to starboard, Bidmean wasn't there. He'd done a bunk. I called him up on the R/T.

'Red two. Report your position.'

His voice indicated he was trembling like an aspen leaf.

'I lost formation, Buster Leader.'

'I am at angels fifteen climbing on a vector of one eight zero. Re-join formation soonest. If you don't, I'll have you court-martialled when we return. The charge will be desertion in the face of the enemy. You'll probably get shot before a firing squad.'

He made no reply. But he knew I meant it. Furthermore, he must have still had the squadron in sight and was waiting his moment to return to base. For it took him only a couple of minutes to return to the squadron. I was climbing directly into the sun and so must he have been.

He didn't try to ram me; he hadn't got the guts for that. He must have been blinded by the sun at the last moment. The nose of a Spitfire suddenly reared into sight in my windshield. It seemed amazingly large for what was a small fighter aircraft. Before it came off my airscrew churned up his fuselage. I was left with a Merlin revving at greatly excessive speed. I had no propeller. The stick was jumping around the cockpit like a hippie at a pop-festival. My Spitfire turned on to its back and I dimly saw Bidmean's aircraft diving vertically minus a tail fin and elevators. I expect that my airscrew had cut his head off in any case. He'd never get out of that alive. I had a slight chance of getting out – if I was lucky.

I jettisoned the cockpit canopy and the jettison system worked. I was suddenly exposed to a 250 mph hurricane and when I tore off my oxygen mask and helmet, the gale blew my cheeks open like a balloon at a fun-fair. I closed my mouth, and my head then didn't try to explode under the pressures. I was still upside down. How fortuitous. I pulled the release pin of the safety harness; the force I used to get the pin undone tore my gauntlets. The Spitfire, still inverted,

91

nosed up thereby applying negative gee and I was catapulted out of the cockpit.

I don't even remember pulling the rip-cord of the parachute. But it opened with a back-breaking jerk. I drifted earthwards like a leaf falling off a catalpa tree in the autumn. I hoped the jagdgeschwader wouldn't spot me. More likely than not they would have shot me in the back. On the way down I brooded and came to a conclusion.

This was the most sensible way to have ended the saga of Bidmean, I thought. Next time up, had he survived this airborne collision (which, incidentally, he did not) he would have done a bunk once again. I would have seen him go and followed him down. Then I would have shot him in the back. What a waste of a Spitfire that would have been. I would have reported that I thought he was a ME 109. Such cases of mistaken identity often occurred in 1940. I wouldn't have been charged with murder.

CHAPTER SEVEN

RANDY

WE all had nick-names on Buster Squadron – Chalky White, Dusty Brown, Dim Black and so on. My surname is Robertson so they called me Randy because the two words alliterated. I wasn't over-sexed, just about average although the average was high. We had a Dirty Watson which doesn't rhyme or anything but he sure was a devil with the women. Mind you, the women rather enjoyed it. Poor little things, young housewives with their husbands away at the war, or innocent little WAAFs who hardly knew what we had in our trousers; but they enjoyed it a lot when they found out. I came over from Canada to try and get a short-service commission in the RAF. I passed my educational and medical tests and was sent to Scone Airport to learn to fly a Tiger Moth in January 1939. Perth was a pleasant town in those days and although I was paid only twelve shillings a day as a civilian pupil pilot under the general authority of the Air Ministry, I could still afford to have a drink or six in the Mess and we shared the cost of taxi rides to Perth. It was only a few miles from the airfield and we drank beer in the pubs, ate cheap meals of fish and chips, and tried it out on some of the wee Scottish lassies, usually with success.

My family originated in Scotland but I am a third generation Canadian. I became an apprentice lumberjack, which was bloody hard work, but I kept looking up at the sky instead of rolling the logs down river. The only place where I could learn to fly was in the UK and through the RAF, so I took a chance with a couple of hundred dollars in my pocket and in due course presented myself at the Air Ministry which was in Adastral House, Kingsway, London. I applied for a short service commission and got my marching orders pretty darned quick after that and found myself back in the country my grandfather left about fifty years before. I went solo on the Tiger Moth after six hours dual, which wasn't bad. Then I see from my pilot's flying log book that I left Scone with 26 hours dual and 27 hours solo.

At Scone we had to attend ground school to learn about things like Vickers machine-guns, which was bloody stupid because Brownings were in service by that time. A retired Warrant Officer explained some of the mechanism and he once said: 'And here gentlemen we have a grub screw. Now you might think that a grub screw is a fuck after lunch, but it isn't. This is a grub screw and its function is so and so.' But I never forgot what a grub screw was or what its function is. He was a darned good instructor as a matter of fact. I've got a record of what they called the Sequence of Instruction for ab initio pilots. It is quite interesting because it really gave one the drill which in the course of time would allow one to fly a Spitfire with a basic knowledge of the mechanical and flying aspects. It reads like this:

1. Air experience for pupil.
2. Effect of controls.
3. Taxiing and handling of engine.
4. Straight and level flying.
5. Stalling, climbing and gliding.
6. Medium turns with and without engine.
7. Taking off into wind.
8. Approaches and landings.
9. Preliminary action in the event of fire including stopping and starting engine.
10. Spinning.
11. First solo.
12. Sideslipping.
13. Further action in the event of fire.
14. Low flying (with instructor only).
15. Steep turns with and without engine.
16. Climbing turns.
17. Forced landings.
18. Landing with and without engine.
19. Instrument flying under hood.
20. Stopping and starting engine in the air.
21. Taking off and landing across wind.
22. Aerobatics.

23. Air navigation.
24. Forced landing test.
25. Cross country test.

I could of course expand on each of these sequences, but
suffice it to say it gave one a darned good preliminary
education as to how to become an operational pilot in due
course. I was always somehow astounded when they handed
me my pay packet every week, because I was not only being
taught to fly for free – why, I was even being paid for it!
One disturbing thing was that I inclined towards air sickness
in the very light Tiger Moths, and at one moment I thought
that my flying instructor would recommend that I be thrown
off the course for this reason, especially when I vomited
during a spin. But he was a good guy and told me to buy
a tin of glucose and that helped a lot. I was never air sick in
heavier aeroplanes but I suspect I would be today if I flew a
light craft in high turbulence.

Then the course dispersed. About twenty-five per cent had
been rejected because they were not proficient enough to go
solo within ten hours which was the dead-line. But a number
of my buddies took the train with me up to Lossiemouth not
far from Inverness for advanced flying training. Scone had
been a casual affair, run by civilians who had retired from
the RAF. We weren't under military discipline there
although we had to conform; we were civilian pupil pilots
financed by the Air Ministry. Lossiemouth was quite
different; it was a regular RAF Station, we were now in
uniform as Acting Pilot Officers and we were subject to
court-martial procedures if we overstepped the mark. By
nature I am a bolshie bastard and I didn't like it at all. We
had to do physical jerks at a hell of an early time in the
morning; we had to form up in squads and jog-trot to the
hangars; and the Staff elected our squad leaders from our
course but by what method God only knows.

I was appointed to a flight and my instructor was a
Sergeant Pilot who had served in a Hurricane squadron, but
he was scared out of his wits about flying. He reacted by
giving me a rough time although I held the King's commission and he didn't – not that that had anything to do with it
at all in reality. My Flight Commander was a little shit who
came from New Zealand and he took an instant dislike to me,

probably because I am over six foot tall and he was about five foot three. He had a terrible inferiority complex and he seized on me as being a good model to help his brain trouble. Every time he could manufacture an excuse, he would put me on a charge and order that I be confined to barracks for a month. This meant that in my spare time I couldn't go riding ponies around the forest rides near Lossiemouth. Why I didn't strangle the bastard I don't know. The best news I ever received was when I learned that he had been shot down over France early in 1940 and I didn't say a prayer for him. He was no bloody good as a pilot anyway. So, in short, my advanced flying training course was not something I like to remember.

This dirty little Kiwi gave me a below average assessment as a pilot on my passing out check and recommended that I be retained at Lossiemouth for three months extra flying training. But I think that the Station Commander had reviewed the situation and he instructed that I be sent to another flight. My new Flight Commander was a hell of a good guy and I guess he had got down wind of the stinking little Kiwi's attitude to me. After only a month he gave me an assessment as an above average pilot and recommended me to be posted to a fighter squadron. Boy, was I glad to see the back end of Lossiemouth.

*   *   *

In this manner I was eventually posted to Buster Squadron which had recently re-equipped from Gauntlets to Spitfires. The squadron commander, Crispin, was a burly man not quite as tall as I am, but he was a hell of a nice guy. He had his office in a tent on an airfield near Cambridge, and he had me in, gave my log book a fleeting glance, and welcomed me to his squadron. This was just before war was declared. He sent me to A Flight and the Flight Commander was quite a nice guy. I was given my own room in the Mess with a bathroom not many yards up the corridor; I was very comfortable, for the first time since I turned to flying. It was surely more comfortable than living as a lumberjack! The set-up was totally pre-war with batmen allocated to junior officers like me and waiters at the dining table; the Mess contained sixty bedrooms and was rather like a palace. The food was good; we ate like horses, and the menu cards had different meals on them every night. All that changed, though, in time. We were lulled by the Phoney War like everybody else. We flew practise sorties engaging in mock attacks that had no relevance to what was to come. The Air Staff and the Staff at Headquarters Fighter Command should really have been put into a gas chamber. They had not the slightest conception of how we should go about things – nor did we for that matter. We were still in the biplane era long after the monoplane fighter was in operational service. This demanded a completely new approach, but we still worked with biplane text-books when we should have been copying the tactics learned by the Luftwaffe over the mountains of Iberia during the Spanish Civil War. We were green cookies all right and it wouldn't take all that long for us to discover that fact for ourselves.

But it was almost pleasurable for me at this period, learning the English way of life – not that it differed all that much from my native British Columbia. In any case, the boys on the squadron kept trying to speak like North Americans because they read thrillers written by people like James Hadley Chase. It wasn't so much that I had to learn to speak English, more that I was their tutor in how to talk like Americans. But I was made to feel immediately at home and I only gave the odd passing thought to my relatives in Canada – although I did write to my mother once a week. It was a great life and when we weren't flying I taught them how to play games like baseball, which they called rounders. I had to change their rules for them, of course. If we weren't on night flying standby, and that was a fairly useless operation even in full moon conditions, we could drive to Cambridge for an evening out. The theory of using Spitfires as night fighters was vague as hell and was only brought about because there were no night fighters. You can only see for about half a mile even in brilliant moon conditions, and the red-hot exhaust stubs on the Spitfire reduced that ability quite a bit. They only showed red at night although they were, of course, also red by day but you couldn't see that.

In theory, British searchlights would cone on to an enemy intruder and when you saw a cone you would fly towards it and shoot down the German. To put it mildly that was a bit of a laugh. What happened in practise to Henry, for example, was that British searchlights coned on his Spitfire.

Then the ack-ack went up to hit the target held by the searchlights, and for once in their lives they did indeed hit the target – the wrong target. Henry managed to get out even though one of his legs was shot right off. Luckily for him he held on to the rip-cord of the parachute after the canopy opened. He realized he was bleeding to death as gushes of blood shot out from his thigh, and that he had better do something about it. He pulled the wire rip-cord around his thigh and screwed it tight as hell so it would act as a tourniquet. That more or less stopped the bleeding and he kept a firm hold on it when he hit the ground and nearly broke his back. God knows how they found him, although it was a bright moon-lit night. His Spitfire hit the deck twenty miles from where he landed. But they found him and patched him up before gangrene set in. That put him off flying for a bit, but they gave him a tin leg and away he went again in the blue sky yonder. He had guts.

Buster Squadron was ordered to re-deploy down in the 11 Group area in August. We were fed up with mucking around with the odd German reconnaissance plane by that time and eager to get into the swing of things. And by God, on my first squadron scramble from an 11 Group base we certainly hit trouble. On that sortie, six of our Spitfires were struck down and three others quite badly damaged. I managed to land with my undercart up, but I had felt the kiss of death on my face. We lost seventy-five per cent of our front line strength in about twenty minutes. It was like bloody murder. We used the wrong tactics, we were heavily out-gunned by the Messerschmitts, it was all a hazy crazy set of circumstances. But very slowly we came to realize what we should do, and despite its light armament the Spitfire was a better fighter than the 109 in most respects. In which context I read and remembered quite a lot of poetry. So it goes like: 'Thither when airmen's bodies fall their eager spirits climb on wings to greet old comrades and recall old days of earthward sojourning.' Or it goes something like that.

I will always remember the day Jim bought it. I was flying as his No. 2 but that didn't help him much, because half a dozen Messerschmitts bounced us. I saw them coming, yelled a warning at Jim over the R/T, climbed like hell and went into a tight turn. Perhaps Jim's R/T had gone unserviceable for he continued straight and level like a zombie at a funeral. One of those German bastards hit Jim's Spitfire hard and it began to burn. I saw him bale out and his parachute open, whereupon he probably passed out from anoxia because we were at 25,000 ft. Then I saw another German bastard diving at Jim and smoke came out of his gun ports. He shot Jim in the back. The Devil then took command of me and I had the advantage of height. I bust the seals on the throttle quadrant to give my Spitfire emergency boost and dived like a bat out of hell. The controls stiffened up so hard at that speed that only a one-time lumberjack would have had the strength to hold the aeroplane. Then I throttled right back else I would have overshot the German. When I was fast on his tail I waited until I was at a range of no more than a hundred yards, because I had to get that bastard; I had to get him. The eight Brownings fired when I pressed the button and there was a sound like a thick carpet being torn apart in the hands of a giant. The dirty rat exploded into a thousand bits. If he had baled out, which he obviously wasn't going to do, I would have taken great pleasure in shooting the bastard in the back while on the end of his parachute.

But Goddamn, I was so close that bits of the Messerschmitt banged all round my Spitfire and wrecked my controls. The joy-stick didn't mean anything any longer; it just jumped around the cockpit like an Indian doing a war dance. I had to get out, but fast, and I worked like an electric eel for that purpose. I floated down and hit the Thames somewhere near Tilbury. Fortunately my Mae-West blew up O.K. and I floated in the water for a half hour until a British MTB picked me up. It got bloody cold towards the end even though it was early September, and there was quite a lot of debris and slicks of oil on the water which kept arriving in my area. But I was O.K., although they checked me out at a naval hospital before releasing me. As for Jim, what the hell is all this talk about the Geneva Convention I want to know.

*   *   *

RANDY might have been given an above average assessment as a pilot, but he should never have been posted to a fighter squadron. He was a bull of a man and could hardly squeeze into the cockpit of a Spitfire. He had that calm kind of fortitude which indicated to me very plainly that he would have made a superb bomber pilot. The normal successful fighter pilot lives on the ends of his nerves, paces the room while he talks, drags away at a cigarette only to throw it away before it's even half-finished. Randy looked like an orang outang and smoked a pipe. He never led a section because he wasn't expert enough to handle a tactical situation, but he was as if made of granite, steadfast in his capacity as a wing-man. Of course, when things got too hot and you had to take violent evasive action, you would lose Randy because his reflexes were none too sharp and his aerobatic ability comparatively slight.

It generally occurred in 1940 that one found oneself alone during and after a skirmish, for the formations we used to fly were totally inadequate against the jagdgeschwarders of the fighter arm of the Luftwaffe. Their tactics were fluid, flexible and lethal. They flew their sections in formations of four Messerschmitts widely spaced so the pilots could give each other mutual protection from attacks from the rear – and most attacks were made from various angles astern. We flew in vics of three Spitfires, four vics to the squadron, assuming we still had twelve Spitfires available for operations, which we normally didn't. Three fighters does not represent a reasonable tactical formation; four do because they can be broken up into the essential fighting unit of two aircraft with their pilots giving each other protection.

I believe that the kill Randy described in his story was the only one he made. Indeed, I was surprised that he lasted as long as he did. British Columbia is in many ways surprisingly like England and the Canadians living there are much more English in their mannerisms than those in the mid-west and most certainly the French Canadians. However, Randy gave me one or two surprises, especially when he introduced me to the art of 'snirging'. What this means is that one watches a pretty girl park her bicycle and walk away, whereupon you go to it and smell the saddle. It was a nauseating practice, but out of curiosity's sake I once 'snirged'. I smelt nothing except saddle leather; perhaps Randy had a keener sense of smell than I.

Even though Randy was a giant of a man he was extraordinarily gentle, both physically and in his drawling speech. A quiet voice issued from those powerful lungs. But the manner of his dying was anything but gentle. He managed to bale out of his burning Spitfire and hit terra firma conveniently near to the plastic surgery hospital near East Grinstead. He was near to death when they recovered him and rushed him in for emergency treatment. Had he survived he would have become automatically a member of the Guinea Pig Club, but he died on the operating table. Richard Hillary suffered similar experiences as he described so vividly in his book The Last Enemy.

'Gradually I realized what had happened. My face and hands had been scrubbed and then sprayed with tannic acid. The acid had formed into a hard black cement. My eyes alone had received different treatment; they were coated with a thick layer of gentian violet. My arms were propped up in front of me, the fingers extended like witches' claws, and my body was hung loosely on straps just clear of the bed.

'I can recollect no moments of acute agony in the four days which I spent in that hospital; only a great sea of pain in which I floated almost with comfort. Every three hours I was injected with morphia, so while imagining myself quite coherent, I was for the most part in a semi-stupor. The memory of it has remained a confused blur.'

We buried Randy with military honours, although we could hardly spare an officer pilot to attend the ceremony. The coffin was extremely heavy because this large man – or corpse – was more or less intact. In retrospect I am glad that Randy died so swiftly. He would have made a very bad guinea-pig.

As Hillary put it: The last enemy that shall be destroyed is death.

CHAPTER EIGHT

PAUL

It was just after the miraculous evacuation of our army from Dunkirk when I joined my fighter squadron. I was particularly thrilled, because I had applied and continued the process from the very first interview with my commanding officer at Initial Training Wing and then throughout my flying training to persuade my superiors to be allowed to fly Spitfire fighters. Before the war I constructed and serviced Spitfires when in the employ of Messrs. Vickers Armstrong, Ltd., because I was an aviation engineer, hence my desire to become a pilot of one of the aircraft I really knew and loved.

After my training I was posted to a Hurricane Operational Training Unit; this might have meant that I would never see a Spitfire squadron, or so I thought. When I was sent on from there, however, it was to a Spitfire squadron. I felt on top of the world, rather like a schoolboy who had just received his first prize at the annual sports day.

I did quite a lot of flying soon after I joined my squadron, practising attacks, learning tactics and generally getting the handling of Spitfires taped. I went to bed one evening as a non-operational pilot. But I was still hoping for the day when I would be classed as operational when I would strut around the squadron dispersal with a Mae West on, with my own ground crew, and my aircraft ready to take off at a moment's notice. The following morning I was awakened at about 3.15 a.m. by an airman, who said, 'Get up, Sarge, you are operational and wanted on readiness at 0345 hours.' I was out of bed like a shot, for the time had arrived for me to really do something. Unfortunately nothing happened that morning. However, in the afternoon we got a scramble order to take off and patrol a merchant convoy proceeding through the Straits of Dover. All was quiet for a while, but just as we were getting bored with loitering over the ships, a message came via the R/T from the controller telling us the Luftwaffe were about to attack the convoy. Everything seemed to happen very quickly after that. Before I had time to appreciate the situation there was a tremendous dog-fight under way. The first thing I knew was that tracer bullets were whizzing past my head, whereupon I acted very quickly. Forgetting all my training, I pulled the aeroplane into a steep, shuddering left turn and climbed into the cloud. Then I emerged from the cloud and saw the Hun just below me and recognized it as a Me 109E. I now had the advantage and dived on him from behind. He saw me and pulled up into the cloud. I waited below in a slow orbit, as I thought he would come out again. The next thing I saw was his aeroplane as a dark shadow coming slowly towards me. I got my sights on the dim form of the 109 and fired my eight guns. It was the first time I had fired all eight guns of a fighter. The result was amazing; the Me 109 just fell out of the cloud like a brick. But the 109 was not the only one to fall out of the sky, for at the same time my aeroplane stalled and started a violent spin to the left. It only did about one and a half turns before I recovered control. Diving down to get flying speed again, I saw several splashes in the sea, after which there seemed to be a series of water spouts all at once. Bombs I thought. By this time I had forgotten all about my Me 109 duel, having seen nothing more of him.

My feelings by this time were a queer mixture of fright, delight at having beaten a 109, and amazement when I then observed the long thin fuselage of a Dornier 17. As I closed up I noticed the dark olive-green camouflage of the German bomber and the large black crosses on a white background. The air above the sea was misty, which made the camouflaged bomber very difficult to discern. Before attacking, as there were no mirrors fitted at that time to our fighters, I did a quick weave to the left and right to ensure that there was nothing on my tail. Then I opened fire at about 250 yards, meeting with considerable opposition from the rear gunner. I got in a good burst before breaking away. I made rather a mess of my break-away and some bullets from what I think was a blister gun on the bomber's port side hit my Spitfire. When I recovered control there was nothing in sight, so I decided to go home to the forward base we were using and land. On the way I took stock of the result of my first combat. The position looked grim to me, for my aircraft was full of holes and pieces of metal were ripping off the wings. On my side I could claim a Me 109 probably destroyed and a damaged Dornier. As I joined the circuit I saw that my airspeed indicator registered 260 mph. I throttled back further but the airspeed indicator failed to respond. To my horror I knew the thing was out of action. What sort of landing would I make? Scared stiff, I came in to land, and to my surprise everything was all right. The engineer officers put my aeroplane unserviceable. I was then flown back to my own base in a light aircraft.

My next sortie was a scramble to intercept some German aircraft performing reconnaissance patrols off Dungeness. I was No. 3 in the leading section of the Flight. We stooged around for about half an hour on various courses given us by the controller. Suddenly we saw a bomber; we had caught our prey. The Hun immediately put his nose down and dived for the sea about 5,000 ft below and at the same time jettisoned his bombs which fell in a large mass, hitting the sea in almost the same form as they left the aircraft. In the meantime the flight commander had ordered us into line astern formation for the attack. This attack was the only perfect attack, as per written instructions, made by any section in which I ever flew. The section-leader went in, fired his guns and broke away. No. 2 did likewise and I then followed. I got in a good burst, with considerable opposition from the rear gunner and all manner of objects were ejected by the enemy, such as pieces of wire, rather like netting from old chicken-runs, and explosive missiles of varying shapes and sizes. Having dodged such objects I found myself going much too fast, and almost collided with the tail of the enemy aircraft. I did a very split-arse breakaway and was terrified in case the front gunner would get a bead on me as I overshot. The next thing I knew was that there was something wrong with my aeroplane, but owing to the thick mist I could see nothing below or above. I took control of myself and lowered my head to gaze at the instruments in the cockpit to sort things out. After what seemed minutes to me I suddenly realized that my aeroplane was upside down. I pulled the stick hard back and completed the bottom half of a loop. Just as I managed to attain a straight and level altitude I saw the water very close; it's difficult to describe my feelings at that moment; to say the least, I was dumbfounded. Instinctively I rammed the throttle full open and pulled back harder on the stick. Fortunately I just missed the water. I climbed up again and flew very sedately back to my base. I was feeling distinctly weak, completely lacking in physical strength. I realized afterwards the obvious thing to have done would have been to roll the Spitfire over right side up, not try and dive it into the sea.

During our waiting periods on the ground we pilots lived in the squadron dispersal hut. There we talked, played games, wrote letters to our relatives, read new orders and discussed our tactics against the crafty Hun. By this method we sorted out the best way to attack various types of German aircraft. The Intelligence Officer was often present and picked up lots of useful information, which the pilots had omitted to tell him in the excited reporting given him on landing. One Intelligence Officer in a squadron I was with was very cunning. When we landed he only wanted to know the number of enemy aircraft destroyed or damaged and nothing more. Later in the day, however, he would come round and get into general conversation with us, by which time the pilot concerned would have had time to think through events involving his last engagement and have a clearer view of what took place, the type of formation adopted by the Huns, the squadron's reaction, and he'd be able to describe precisely the type of dog-fight that took place. This method was favoured by the pilots, for it enabled them to fill in a combat report later in the day very much more accurately than would have been possible immediately after landing.

We had pictures of various kinds hanging around the dispersal hut. Glorious women in the scantiest of clothing; silhouettes of German aircraft; charts showing gun positions and arcs of fire, which meant how many degrees the German rear-gunner could move his guns to aim at attacking fighters. In addition we had drawings of don't's and do's issued by Fighter Command Headquarters. One of these pictures showed a pilot diving on his girl-friend's house, giving the neighbourhood a thrill, but omitting to notice a pylon close to the house; this he unfortunately hit after one of his low dives. Such pictures are far better than tons of bumf, for they show the real thing, thus impressing on every person the danger of such beat-ups. I frequently used to go out and talk to the ground crew who serviced my aeroplane. This I found to be a very good policy, for by so doing one got to know the capabilities of the men and it also gave them an interest and something more to work for. A chat with the fitter about the engine and its performance helped him quite a lot in diagnosing minor faults without putting the aircraft unserviceable. The rigger also liked to know how the aeroplane flew and if he could improve its qualities. Every pilot liked to have his flying kit in a certain position in the cockpit, so if you went along and told the crew just how you preferred to have your helmet and gloves positioned, the parachute either in the pilot's seat with the straps in a convenient position, or on the tailplane so that the fitter could be starting the engine whilst the pilot was getting his parachute on, this all made for good team work which is essential in a speedy scramble. If we took more than three minutes to get the whole squadron into the air the squadron-commander tended to use strong language.

One thing that would have been very impressive if the public could have seen it, I'll endeavour to describe. Assume the squadron was at immediate readiness, the ground crews by the aircraft and pilots in the dispersal hut. The telephone would ring, every pilot would unstiffen his knees ready to dash to his aeroplane. Betty, the WAAF driver of our Humber brake would start the engine, ready to take pilots who had a long way to go round to their aircraft. But the message might be something to do with the weather forecast, which was quite unnecessary as we had all looked out of the window and knew very well what sort of weather was likely. Everybody relaxed again and our disc-jockey would put on another Bing Crosby record, to everybody's delight. Again the phone would ring. We would prepare for a scramble and I would pop a piece of chewing-gum in my mouth. Chewing-gum is a great help when flying, I think; it keeps the saliva up and prevents a dry feeling in the back of one's throat which pure oxygen tends to produce. But such telephone calls might come only from the steward in the sergeants' mess who wanted to know how many late dinners to keep warm. Betty, a plump little thing with large brown eyes and semi-bleached hair, would switch off the engine of the brake as the pilots relaxed. We would start to play table tennis. The telephone would screech again. This time it was the real thing. 'Buster Squadron scramble! Patrol Dover-Dungeness angels twenty-five!' The telephone operator yelled to the nearest ground crews through the window, 'Start up'. In a few seconds every engine burst into life. Betty departed with her load of pilots. She was a good driver and knew where to stop for each pilot. We were all in our cockpits and our straps were done up quicker than you could say knife. The fitter's last words as I taxied out were 'The oxygen is on, Sarge; best of luck.'

We would taxi out manoeuvring ourselves into pre-arranged sections of three. We took off six at a time. No sooner had the first flight got half-way across the aerodrome than the second flight opened up for take-off. We climbed on an interception course aimed at German raiders flying in to bomb shipping in Dover Harbour. The controller told the C.O. to go flat out, and he did. We got to the coast and saw nothing, having climbed all the way. We didn't get to 20,000 ft because we would then have been above the cloud. No German could bomb a convoy from above the cloud. We, that is my section, were ordered to climb through the cloud to see what was around up there and report to the C.O. who was patrolling under the cloud, ready to pounce on any enemy aircraft that came down through the cloud in search of the convoy. My section consisted of three aircraft. We climbed up through about 3,000 ft of thick cloud as fast as maybe. When we penetrated the cloud we arrived in lovely sunshine. It's a wonderful sight to see the sun shining on the billowy clouds below, though we didn't on this occasion have time to enjoy it, for as we got about 500 ft above the cloud and had time to look around, dive-bombers, which we identified as Ju 87s, were commencing to dive through the cloud to attack the ships. We wheeled to starboard after them and at the same time got jumped by a number of Me 109s from above. The third man of our section was considerably more crafty than the other two of us. He climbed higher than we did before turning to dive on the bombers. In so doing he saw the escort fighters whizz past him to attack us. Next thing I knew was that four 109s were diving at me. I rolled my Spitfire on to its back and went straight down.

Two of the 109s followed me. This was where our No. 3 saved the situation, for he dived on the 109s. Their pilots were scared stiff, because they didn't know how many Spitfires were coming down at them from behind. His tactics were well repaid, for the bombers were either shot down or so badly disorganized that the bombs were dropped into the water, not one of the ships being touched. The squadron claimed about six Ju 87s destroyed, and a Hurricane squadron arrived to guard the ships against further attacks; we then returned to our base.

Aerial attacks on convoys were becoming the rule, consequently we had the job of patrolling convoys fairly regularly. It's a binding job while there is nothing doing, just stooging up and down over the convoys and getting more fed-up each time. Readiness would be at 4 o'clock in the morning. Some of the pilots had slept at dispersal and others would roll up from the messes in the shooting-brake looking tired. Our working hours were long in those days, usually from first light to dusk; even into the night in full moon conditions. Our flying kit would be put in our respective aeroplanes by the ground crews, who had already run up the engines to full power and checked everything and reported to the flight-sergeant. The telephone would ring. Would the Squadron Commander speak to the Controller? There was a convoy off Beachy Head and we had to supply one section to fly over it until 9 a.m. when a Hurricane squadron from the same aerodrome would take over from us. Off went the first section of three aircraft. I was usually in the first section and stooged along economizing on fuel as far as possible once we reached the convoy. We would fly over it first to let the sailors see we were friendly, then proceed to introduce ourselves to each ship in turn. We flew very low over and round the ships as they steamed on their zigzag courses. The crews would wave all manner of queer things at us. I remember on one particular occasion, from a deck-house of a small ship there emerged a very fat man wearing only a pair of trousers and a vest. He put the bucket he was carrying on the end of a broom and started waving. Others waved caps, shirts and any old thing they could get hold of. Apparently they enjoyed the security we were supposed to give them, for each convoy would greet us in a similar way.

Our patrols lasted for approximately an hour and then

another three fighters would take over from us. By about noon the ships would be nearing Dover. This brought the convoys into the danger zone, so instead of having one section on patrol there would be probably three or four squadrons near the ships. The Luftwaffe would arrive in the form of Me 109s to try and split up the British escort fighters, then about ten minutes later would come the bombers. Some of the best dog-fights I have been involved in developed in a few seconds. No time to think any more, for aeroplanes would be whizzing round in small circles and tracer bullets flying in all directions. Suddenly I saw an aeroplane burst into flames and go down like a stone. I then spotted a nice juicy bomber about to attack an isolated ship; down I dived after him. Another Spitfire followed me. We both hesitated before attacking. I had never seen a German bomber like that before. I broke away to have a look at the markings. Sure enough, the black crosses were there, but I recognized the machine as a French Chance-Vaught bomber. We shot it down into the sea between us. The other pilot turned out to be my Flight Commander. Another bit of information for the Intelligence Officer – the Huns were using French aircraft they had captured. Suddenly all was quiet. The battle was over. I decided to have a look round the ships before going home. The convoy had scattered and one ship was down at the stern. I wondered if any of the crew were hurt.

On the way back to base I thought about the scrap we had just had. The results from a German standpoint seemed to be very poor compared with the number of fighters and bombers the Luftwaffe had sent over to sink our ships. I was last back and was getting quite a reputation for being the last home. My crew wanted to know what happened, so I gave them a brief outline. They then set to work to get my Spitfire ready in the shortest possible time. I joined the other pilots and we had our customary chat about our last combats; the Flight-Commander informed the Intelligence Officer about his attack on the French aircraft and I was able to assist him and make it known that I was with him when he attacked. Then we retired to the dispersal hut for refreshment; our Intelligence Officer had ordered coffee to be brewed for our return. The Flight-Sergeant very soon after entered the shack to say all aircraft were refuelled and ready to take the air, and almost immediately I was airborne again to relieve the Hurricanes over the convoy. Nothing happened this time, so we returned after our hour's patrol without incident.

The Huns then began to blitz our forward bases and we had several clashes with the enemy farther inland. Then the Battle of Britain really started. I'll never forget the first time I saw the Germans coming to attack our inland aerodromes. We were flying at about 15,000 ft when we saw the Huns, they looked rather like a swarm of bees in flight, one solid mass of bombers surrounded by whirling fighters. Bombers in the middle, hordes of fighters all round them; some in close formation and others spread out over the sky. I felt very lonely and very much afraid at first; there seemed to be only twelve of us against all that number. Of course there were plenty of other British squadrons airborne but I couldn't see them at the time; anyway we carried on and went straight through the balbo head-on. It was a strange experience as the large black bombers swept over our heads and underneath us in their efforts to dodge head-on collisions. To be quite frank, I really don't know how we all got away without a great number of mid-air collisions.

As I turned my head I could see the result of our first encounter with the large formation of Huns; they had split up and we took advantage of the position. The Messerschmitt pilots seemed to be so shocked that they didn't get cracking for a bit, but very soon dog-fights were developing all over the sky; I imagine the result would be similar if wasps and bees were mixed up in a fight. As soon as I saw the balbo split I forgot my fear and selected a big long Flying Pencil as target. He thereupon jettisoned his bombs and turned for home. I chased him, attacked several times and eventually saw him belly-land in a field near the coast. I was again on top of the world, for it was my first single-handed confirmed victory. I circled over the enemy and took my map from the holder to mark the spot where he crashed. I then proceeded to beat the sod up. As I came down in my first dive I saw the pilot climb out, and as I pulled up I looked back at the big black object on its belly in the field, the crew all prisoners of war. One was injured, for I could see the crew carrying him away from the aeroplane. I dived again. This time the pilot, who seemed little interested in the other crew, shook his fist at me and threw his life-jacket viciously on the ground. I saw a farmer walking across to the machine with a sporting gun held in his right hand.

I flew back to base and I heard the controller telling all aircraft to be extremely careful on landing. When I arrived over my airfield and took note of its condition I thought the controller a perfect optimist. I couldn't see a place at first on which to land, there were so many bomb craters. However, I studied the position and decided to land on one runway with a large crater about two-thirds of the way down it. I juggled the aircraft in safely, feeling greatly relieved as I had hardly enough petrol to go farther. To my amazement there was a Spitfire in the crater on the runway; it contained one of Buster Squadron's pilots. His windscreen had stopped a direct hit which had also shattered some of the perspex canopy and cut his face. He couldn't see where he was going after landing and consequently finished in the crater. It was pretty hazardous trying to keep going with an airfield filled with craters; there were several delayed-action bombs which might explode at any time and I wondered what would happen if one burst when I was taxiing with the wing right over the little mound which signified there was a bomb, unexploded, below.

Despite such difficulties we managed to continue to react to the scramble order though our take-off time was considerably lengthened, as may well be imagined. I remember on one very hot day the squadron was sent off to intercept masses of German aircraft at about noon. One of our pilots, who was returning from forty-eight hours' rest, reached the gates of the Station just as the Tannoy announced that a raid was imminent and would all available pilots please take up any aircraft they could find to help defend the aerodrome. Our returned pilot nipped smartly over the hedge, grabbed a Mae West, parachute, and helmet, and took my aeroplane, which had been declared unserviceable but had been repaired. I was flying his aeroplane. He took off, intercepted a Hun bomber near our base, shot it down, and returned to the aerodrome for more ammunition, all in the space of twenty minutes. (Incidentally his leave was not up until 1 p.m. that day). Just outside the aerodrome we later found his destroyed Dornier 17 in a field on its belly.

After we were released that night, which was about 11 p.m. we got some of our fitters to cut out one of the large crosses off the Dornier and hang it in the mess. There it acted as a fire-screen for a long time. Then the Luftwaffe turned its attention to London. We continually intercepted the raiders; I often thought of my girl friend who was probably at that moment hurrying to a shelter from the office in which she was employed. I used to catch glimpses of a few crafty sods breaking up, turning for home, and then a few seconds later about-turning their bombers towards London. It was my ambition to fire at one of these types and explode his bombs for him. One day I almost succeeded in doing it. I got underneath and to the sun side on a Ju 88; I then throttled back and waited for the raider to get just a little ahead so I could aim accurately at him. However, my luck was out, for just as I pressed the gun button he dropped the load of bombs. I was furious, so proceeded to get him down anyway. This I managed to do successfully, though since I was sitting too close behind after using all my ammunition, having put the rear gunner and both engines out of action, one of the gunners suddenly opened fire at me. He was a good shot too. One of his bullets went through my perspex cockpit canopy, hit the side of my helmet and went out of the back. Another single bullet entered my port wing and made everything inside unserviceable. Another lesson learnt. Never wait in range for your victim to crash.

By this time I was becoming very tired; I could keep my spirits up if I was flying, but as soon as I came down I was scared of being bombed on the ground. We had a dose of bombing one evening at about six o'clock. We had just landed, six of us, and our oxygen bottles were being recharged and the aeroplanes refuelled. Everybody was brassed-off. We had been up about four times that day and seen nothing. We had the radio on in the dispersal hut and were listening to the news. After this one of our sergeant-pilots was going to broadcast. He had shot down five 109s in a day and was going to tell the listeners of his experiences. But the controller rang up and asked if we were ready to scramble. We couldn't; our machines were still being serviced. He told us to get into the air raid shelters quick as hell. We took a very dim view, but had no time to argue. As we looked out of the door of the hut an airman said to me 'look at all those Blenheims, Sarge'. I ordered him into the shelter, for they were enemy bombers which then proceeded to drop their bombs all over the airfield. Everyone of us decided we would much rather fly with hundreds of Huns around than be bombed on the ground. When bombs start to fall I always have a feeling of utter frustration and fear; I suppose it's because one is so helpless on the ground.

Towards the end of the Battle of Britain I had landed from a sortie and my Spitfire was unserviceable because one of the guns had jammed. There was no other aircraft available for me and the armourers were busy when the order to take off was given. Owing to the distance that the aircraft had to be dispersed, I was in the habit of riding my bike to my aeroplane. I cycled as fast as I could to see if there was a possibility of getting airborne with one gun out of action. The Sergeant armourer said 'I only want a new gun-barrel, and then you can go.' I sent him off for one on my bike. Unfortunately he gave two or three very hard shoves on the pedals and the chain broke. He and bike were all mixed up in a heap on the grass, so he raced off on foot and returned in somebody's car. By this time the squadron was taking off. Optimistically I strapped myself in the cockpit. By the time I was ready he had repaired the machine-gun; it took just two minutes to fit. I chased after the squadron, and eventually caught them up, just in time to intercept some He 111s almost over the aerodrome. We came up behind them this time and couldn't get anywhere near for ack-ack fire. The squadron commander requested the controller to order the guns to cease firing, which they did, but the bombers were by then getting mighty close to Tilbury Docks. We went in to attack from straight behind. This is a dangerous practice when there are a number of bombers together because the fire from the rear gunners is terrific. However, we thought the risk was worth it. Four of us went in to attack whilst the others remained behind to ward off any Me 109s. The four of us attacked in line abreast formation to confuse the gunners. The result was good as the bombers split up and jettisoned their bombs. The rest of the squadron then attacked. I think nearly everybody got something that day and it all happened over the aerodrome where our ground personnel should have been in the air raid shelters; but not they; they knew their squadron was in action above them.

I remember one Hun just breaking up and coming down in flames very close to the airfield under the withering fire of one of the Flight Commanders. I got one too. It was one of the runaway ones. I did my usual form of attack and stopped his port engine. The other wouldn't seem to stop – it only slowed up and the under-carriage came hanging down in a limp fashion. That was the best indication I got that he was done for. We were well above cloud at the time I made my attack and I was afraid I would lose my victim in cloud. The cloud was the alto-cumulus type which pleased me, as I could keep an eye on him. One has plenty of time to think when just waiting for an aeroplane to glide down. I kept at a safe distance and tried to picture myself in their shoes. Prisoners, I thought; they'll probably be much happier here in prison than fighting a war. I decided it would be the best place for them anyway. I thought of the gunner and wondered if he was dead. I learned afterwards he was. We got lower and lower. I saw an aerodrome below. The Hun turned and I thought he was going to crash in a wood. But he used his crippled engine and just got over the wood. But crashed on the aerodrome. I went down and beat him up, of course. I hadn't a single bullet left, and wouldn't have used it if I had. I spent the last 1,000 ft dodging ground-defence fire. The blighters on the aerodrome opened fire at the Hun but missed him and nearly shot down two or three of us, for several Spitfire and Hurricane pilots had flown to the scene to see the crash. I didn't land at that airfield but thought I would hurry back to base, because I felt sure some of the other pilots would claim that they shot the Hun down. I was rewarded for my trouble, because I got the victory confirmed. Incidentally one of our pilots had his engine put out of action by the first lot of ack-ack fire, but he landed safely in a field near one of the batteries; I'll leave you to guess what he said to them.

After the Battle of Britain we had to act in defence against the fighter menace. Higher and higher we had to go, in order to get top sides of the Hun. It's a rather lonely feeling to be very high in the sky with such worries to contend with. Patrol at 30,000 ft was the common order. It is very cold up there and the windscreen and hood freeze up at the slightest suspicion of moisture. We would run into batches of 109s at various heights, we might either jump them or they would jump us. Dog-fights at fantastic speeds would develop, and in these it was the best pilot who won the day. When stooging along, breathing only oxygen, and not being able to see much owing to a frosty hood, I always felt that the Luftwaffe pilots were in the worst position and had to fly an aeroplane that was considerably more troublesome at those heights than our Spitfires. It was just a battle of wits, with little result. I became brassed off with such continual high flying, but one got used to it after a time; it is a very exhausting pastime. I remember on one occasion, four of us climbed about seven miles high and chased nine 109s to the coast. Our contrails must have been unusual, for in the daily papers next day there were photographs of our trails. I'm sure if the public who looked at them had realized that it took about an hour to thaw our hands when we got down, they would have been sorry such beautiful photos had been taken.

Ring-twitch* was common among the pilots, but not one admitted it. Then one day I got the wrong end of a 109. He was a very crafty sod, and what is more he had bags of guts. He attacked me all on his own, when I was flying with two squadrons. I didn't see him at all. My mirror and hood were frozen. All of a sudden I heard over the radio, 'Look out!' I hadn't time. He had fired as the words of warning were spoken. He got me but not all of me. I was out of action for some months after crashing, luckily on an aerodrome. The more I think of the life of a fighter pilot, the more I think that luck plays a big part. That Hun had every advantage, and had he been a more accurate marksman or not got scared at the last moment, I should not be writing this story. I'm only waiting to get another crack at the Hun, and when I do, I hope it's a nice fat juicy bomber all to myself. I consider the loss of one German bomber worth two fighters for several reasons. It takes longer to build them, costs more money, entails more labour, and we get at the minimum three of their airmen at one go – a point well worth remembering.

* * *

PAUL was a Sergeant Pilot on Buster Squadron and learned to fly with the Volunteer Reserve before the war. He didn't know how to write, but notwithstanding he should have been given a commission; he wasn't, because the staffs weren't doing their job properly. Paul looked like Mr. Pick-

* 'Ring-twitch' means fear of going into combat.

wick, short, dumpy, rotund, pink-cheeked, cheerful; and he was undersexed. He should have been a parson not a fighter pilot; he'd have been trustworthy enough with the Communion wine.

Paul had worked with the Supermarine Aircraft Company before the war as he explained, had assisted in producing the inadequate flow of Spitfires off the production lines, and he knew more about the Spitfire than our senior Flight Sergeant Fitter Airframe. One pint of beer was enough to get Paul drunk, even give him a hang-over in the morning, so it didn't cost much when we took him out to the pubs. There was no differential in 1940, of course, between officer and sergeant pilots. They never called us 'Sir' but they did salute first thing in the morning because they were saluting the King's Commission not the man who wore the officer's uniform.

In retrospect it seems a crazy situation, but it worked all right in 1940. Officer pilots, so to speak, commanded Sergeant pilots on the ground, but Sergeant Pilots could and did command officer pilots in the air. The leader of a section was selected for his flying experience not by rank. In 1940 something like thirty-five per cent of the total number of pilots in Fighter Command were NCOs. Most of these had been creamed off from the RAF Apprentices' School at Halton near Wendover. Competition to be accepted into that technical college was fierce and pretty high standards of education were a sine qua non. To float to the top of the sediment at Halton and be preferred for pilot training meant you had to be good, very good. I was under command of a NCO pilot when we shared the kill of my first Hun, a Dornier 17 – we termed it the Flying Pencil.

As a digression from the theme, and the theme is Paul, the Germans preferred to work in the milieu of a kind of mob hysteria, whereas Britons were loners. The Luftwaffe generals took advice from psychiatrists when designing their bombers. They were informed that bomber crews would retain their morale best if they were all contained within touching distance. Accordingly, the Do 17, He 111 and Ju 88 were all designed with air crews operating close to the pilots' seats, within touching distance. The system worked very well as a matter of fact. The staffs in the British Air Ministry were possessed of no such sensibility. The rear-gunner of a

116

Wellington, or a Halifax, or a Lancaster was ten yards from human contact. Not only was he frozen blue, he was also the first to die. If, in fact, the pilot's cabin blew up and his inter-com was severed, the rear-gunner would be stuck in his coffin without realization.

To revert to Paul: he died of course. 'Killed in action' was the verbiage used by the Air Ministry when they sent the fatality signal to his parents. Paul should have appreciated that he was pretty useless as a fighter pilot; he should have realized that his reflexes weren't sharp enough, that he was not possessed of the murderer's instinct which is essential when you have to shoot a German pilot in the back.

So, go, lovely roses, rosy cheeks too. One day in the Spring of 1941 Paul swept the skies over Holland from a base in East Anglia. He looked at the fenland with its marvellous visibility which gave Rembrandt and Vermeer the in-spiration to perform miracles with their paints 400 years before Paul died. Perhaps he was gazing at Haarlem not in his rear-view mirror; perhaps he was thinking of Franz Hals who was born in Haarlem; perhaps he wasn't thinking. He was bounced by a couple of Me 109s each equipped with two 20 mm cannon and various machine-guns and they shot him in the back. His Spitfire exploded and fell like the autumn foliage into the Zuyder Zee.

So did what was left of Paul. Technically, he was what we termed a flamer.

CHAPTER NINE

RUFUS

IT was going to be a magnificent day. First light had just given sufficient visibility to show the outlines of small cumulus clouds, but there was some time to sunrise and it was cool. There had been heavy dew overnight and as I plodded over to my Spitfire, not much more than a silhouette on the skyline, the dew on the grass made my flying boots wet; I only hoped it wouldn't soak into the fleece lining. Then my feet would ice up at 35,000 ft and I might die of frostbite as opposed to getting a bullet in my back.

The crew were there, busy checking over the aircraft after the first engine run. The air frame rigger, Walsh, came forward, took my parachute and laid it on the wing. The engine fitter, Davies, came round and told me she was in good trim. A grand pair they were to have as a crew; they kept that Spitfire spotless both inside and out; if there was just one thing wrong with her, the slightest hint of trouble, they'd put in hours of extra work to track the fault down. Strange to think that on these two men and a few others one's life depended. If they made mistakes or forgot to do something, then the Spitfire might pack up during a combat – if not before.

After our usual chat I climbed into the Spitfire and checked over the instruments and controls, then signed the form 700. Yes, they'd topped up with petrol after the morning run-up. Everything was set for the coming day. I walked back to the dispersal hut. Most of the others were there, putting on their Mae Wests and making last-minute adjustments to their varied flying clothing.

I was set fair to come to immediate readiness, so I flopped into the nearest chair. My feet and hands were cold, but there wasn't any heat coming from the fire. The squadron pilots were not exactly in a party mood. Somehow, there's not much to say at 4.30 in the morning; it's later, just before breakfast, when they begin to talk about their sexual experiences the night before, if any.

Every now and then, the bloody field telephone bell would ring and everyone would try to catch the gist of the conversation. The sector operations controller was the normal offender, making a few inquiries or passing on some information. Up to date, it appeared that there were no plots of any interest on the ops. table. A few Huns out on reconnaissance had been reported, but they were well out to sea. One or two of the pilots had dropped off into an uneasy doze; and now and then there would be a few muttered words between the others; or someone would get up and look out of the window, maybe open the door and step outside. Their average age was about twenty-one; I was an old man in comparison. Since we moved south into the blitz area, there had been quite a few changes in the half-dozen or so that came with us. The others – well, they're either dead or in hospital. There was only one who was posted from the squadron – his nerves couldn't stand the racket. I found it interesting to speculate as to what was going on in their minds; did they think and feel the same way about things as I did; were they standing the strain better than myself? There was no doubt that it was tough going. We flew most of the daylight hours, had little time off and were obliged to snatch meals as and when we could. As for sleep, that was reduced to a point where one felt exhausted by mid-morning, with more than the average man's working day still ahead of us. But we had a big job to do and by God we'd see it through or go to hell, every man Jack.

Young Joe was in bad shape this morning. I hoped we wouldn't have too bad a day for his sake. He badly needed a rest from operations but there was no one to replace him. Time dragged by, the sun was beginning to rise and with it little swirls of ground mist rose from hollows in the terrain. Bill was busy writing a letter, most probably to that girl friend he'd told me about; Tim was happily sleeping, snoring like an old sow; Joe was tying and untying knots in a piece of string; Butch was just looking straight ahead, thinking no doubt; but from his expression you couldn't tell, his eyes were glazed.

Just at this moment the phone bell went again. As usual, everyone became silent, motionless, straining to catch the words before they were spoken. Then, from the answers and expression on the face of the airman who manned the telephones it was obviously the scramble order. There was a scraping of chairs and then a general rush for the door. A yell from one of the pilots sent the ground crews racing to the Spitfires, closely followed by the pilots. Within a few moments of that shout, the first engine started up with a roar, breaking the quiet of a summer's morning; within seconds, the Merlins in all twelve Spitfires were running. There was a short lull as the pilots strapped themselves into their seats, then the Spitfires were taxiing out as fast as was prudent. The sun had risen fairly high by now and the morning mists had almost cleared. As I taxied to the take-off point I saw the sparkle of the sun on the grass reflected by the dewdrops. Somehow one can't help wondering in these last moments of earthliness with all the beauties of nature around, just how many pilots will ever see them again. As I taxied out I said as always a wee prayer – 'Please God help us all.' With well-practised drill, the pilots lined up at the take-off point; with a wave of the hand by the leader, we opened our throttles for take-off. Twelve Spitfires leapt forward gaining speed; up came their tails and away we climbed, circling the airfield for a short while until we had formed up, then we swung east, climbing at maximum boost.

All this time I had been working hard; taxiing takes up one's attention. Taking off and getting into your allotted position is more automatic and as I did so I looked at the two pilots on my wings, Joe to right and Butch to left. They were both busy doing things inside their cockpits but suddenly Butch looked up. His oxygen mask and helmet hid most of his face. I knew he gave me one of those quick sheepish smiles of his, just as he sometimes did when we were back on the deck. Then we got on with the business in hand.

Up and up we circled, the broken cumulus cloud was at about 12,000 ft, beautifully outlined by the blue sky above; the cloud flashed by as we climbed beyond. It was getting appreciably colder and I was feeling hungry. I turned my oxygen on to emergency and took two deep breaths; I had been feeling the lack of it for the past couple of minutes. Then I turned it back to normal. I wondered what this sortie would bring with it – not as bad as it was yesterday, I hoped.

I turned my oxygen on after another 1,000 ft and looked round my instruments. We were climbing fast, but the oil and coolant temperatures were normal. I switched on my gun-sight, turned the safety catch on the gun button to fire and went through all the other checks automatically. The fighter controller hadn't had much to say since we took off. Appar-ently there were a dozen or more Huns allegedly floating around somewhere near Dungeness. They were supposed to be at some twenty-five or thirty thousand feet, so we con-tinued to climb flat out. Up to 32,000 ft then, in order to gain the advantage of the sun, we swept off towards the east. Down below, like a plasticine model, I could see the whole of the south-east of England, and on the other side of the Channel, France. But somehow not the France I'd been to so often before the war; this was a nasty, dark, gloomy France. This was only due to the cloud formation over land, but it did somehow seem symbolic. We crossed the English coast and circled out to sea, coming in towards Dungeness, hoping to catch the Hun unawares. Everybody's eyes were straining, straining for those little black dots that meant – who knew what?

We were still flying at maximum speed. The controller told us that the Huns had turned for home. If we met them it would most probably mean a head-on attack and I must say I'm not keen on the idea of a head-on with the 109. I don't particularly mind machine-guns, but I've a great deal of respect for that cannon – it pushes out nasty big chunks of high-explosive missiles, and only the other day I saw what it could do when Ron came back with three hits on his machine. Butch caught my eye at that moment and gave me a wave – that wave expressed everything. Still no sign of the bloody Germans though. We were well over Dungeness by now, not quite but almost up sun; if we were ever going to meet them, now was the ideal time. Buster Squadron's pilots were all straining their eyes like hell to catch just a fleeting glimpse of those black dots; one of us could then give the warning and everybody would train his eyes in the right direction. I was just telling myself that we had missed them when there was a yell of 'Tally Ho' on the R/T. I scanned the whole horizon in one quick flash. Still I couldn't see them, but while I was wondering where they could be, the squadron commander wheeled to port and then settled down on steady course. We were going flat out now, diving slightly towards France. I searched virtually every square inch of the sky and I'm damned if I could see a thing.

On we went, streaking down at full throttle, and suddenly, just as I thought the squadron commander had the DTs, there they were! I'll never be quite certain whether there were twelve or fourteen – they were rather spread out. For once we were going to have the jump on them, that is, if we could catch them up, for they also were flying at maximum boost. They'd got a good start on us, but I don't think they knew we were so close to them. Very gradually, we were overtaking them. We still had plenty of height over them. The rate of the dive increased; we were losing height rapidly now and closing range fast. Just as I thought we'd managed to bag a sitting target for once, with only about 500 yards to go one of the Huns must have seen us, for like a flash the formation broke up, diving in all directions. A quick order came on the R/T and each of us picked his own particular Hun. Mine jammed his stick forward and went down in, as near as damn it, a vertical dive. We were now at 23,000 ft. I lost sight of him under the nose of my Spitfire but I soon got him in view again. Down and down we went; hell, my eardrums were hurting. It was no good; he was travelling faster than me; I was going to lose him. My only hope was to do him in as he pulled out of the dive. I turned slightly off his track and got out to one side. I daren't look round and see if anything was following me, because I knew if I took my eyes off him for a second, he would disappear. Somehow or other, they always vanish against the sea. Their camouflage was very good. Down and down he went. I got the awful feeling that the blighter might not pull out in time for me to get a squirt at him but just dive into the sea. I was doing something near 500 mph. How the hell he hoped to pull out at that speed I'd no idea. He appeared to be absolutely on the water. I expected to see him crash at any second, but I was wrong – somehow he did pull out, slowly, but quite surely. I suppose he looked dead behind him to see if I was still there. That is where the sucker made his first and really last mistake. I was well up on his left, and as near as I could judge, directly up sun as far as he was concerned. I waited a few seconds before I put in my attack, to make quite sure as to whether he had seen me or not. Apparently not, for he had throttled back and seemed to be taking it quite easy. If he looked back it was only directly behind him. I turned in and gingerly felt for the firing button. Down I went. Still he hadn't seen me. It was his last moment of breathing. For the second after he saw me, my rounds hit him. He had been right down on the water-level – I pumped him full of lead. For a few seconds he flew dead straight and suddenly, without any warning, pulled right up and climbed until he reached the vertical – he was finished. Flames were coming from underneath the Messerschmitt and he was leaving a big trail of black smoke. I didn't try and follow him – when he came down would be time enough, if by any chance he was not a dead goose. He climbed up to 500, perhaps 750 ft, then went on to his back and dived straight down into the water. There was a hell of a splash and that was that. Just nothing left. I circled the spot for a while to see if anything rose to the surface, not that I really expected anything. After the bubbles had ceased, all that was left of the German pilot and his 109 was a patch of oil. No good hanging around.

I was then about half-way across the Channel. We'd used a hell of a lot of petrol chasing this particular batch and I had to be getting back. I turned towards England and let my thoughts wander, although I kept a wary eye open in case some Hun spotted me. I'd been lucky that time, it had been a pushover; none of his colleagues had followed me down. If only they were all as easy as that. I throttled back to the most economical cruising speed. I hadn't got much petrol left, and if I was not careful I'd have to land and refuel before I could get back to my base. God forbid that I should have to do that! It was just on breakfast-time and I was as ravenous as a wolf.

When I arrived back over my airfield another Spitfire was landing, so I did a circuit. Then down I went. As I taxied in to the dispersal, I quickly counted the squadron aircraft. Perhaps they hadn't all landed yet. Yes, there was another one coming in now. I shut down the engine and climbed out as I did so, the crew and armourers leapt on the wings. I hadn't fired very much, only about 115 rounds per gun, but I was pretty short of petrol; only seven gallons were left. I told the crew what had happened as they began to refuel the Spitfire, then wandered off towards the dispersal hut. There were still three who hadn't landed. No good worrying about them. I had to have my breakfast and be back at readiness as quickly as possible. It was going to be yet another busy day.

Just as we were half-way through breakfast, a message came through that we needn't hurry. Things had died down for the time being and we could take it easy; we'd be called when necessary. Nevertheless, we all ate our breakfast as quickly as possible; one never knew how soon it might be necessary. I was just getting up to go, when our Intelligence Officer came in and said two of our 'missing' pilots had landed at other aerodromes to refuel as they had had long chases across the Channel. But one was obviously and truly missing. Apparently our net bag for this first sortie was five.

Then I hurried to my room in the mess for a shave but we were suddenly called to readiness again. I wiped the lather off the other side of my face and rushed out of the mess, only just in time to catch the squadron lorry. We jog-trotted to our aircraft when the lorry dumped us at the dispersal as the scramble order had already come through. I clambered into the Spitfire and strapped myself in tightly. It was the same sort of patrol. Apparently Kesselring had sent some more Messerschmitts over South-Eastern England but they were flying much higher this time. The sun was well up by now and the grass was as near as damn it bone dry; all the dew had disappeared. As we taxied out, the dust began to rise. Yes, it was exactly the same as yesterday and the day before. We lined up into position. Where the hell was that other fellow? There should have been ten Spitfires; somehow there were only nine. We roared into the air and as we circled the airfield I looked down and saw one of the Spitfires still in its dispersal position. There was a small batch of men standing around it; something had gone wrong.

In spite of the fact that it had been quite warm when we took off, it was pretty darned cold at height. When we got to 32,000 ft we levelled out. We'd flown north-east in order to get the best results out of the sun, but it didn't much matter now, for the Hun had it in his favour the whole time. We turned south and again started out across the Channel; then, when in mid-Channel, we turned again and started sweeping down the Channel. Yes, there they were way over to starboard; I could see the vapour trails. They were high, all right, most probably 34,000 ft. We didn't turn towards them at once. We started climbing and hoped to heaven that we'd be able to cut them off, but somehow or other, I didn't think we could. They were travelling at a hell of a speed and we'd have to make up at least another 2,000 ft to get at them. After what seemed hours (but was probably only three or four minutes) we were almost up to them, but they were still above us. We had started making contrails ourselves now, so they couldn't help but see us. We started turning towards them; it was no good, we couldn't intercept them before they passed over us, so we turned again and flew along on a parallel course. With a bit of luck, they'd come down to have a pot at us and we'd get away without too much damage. Not a bit of it, the yellow rats kept on flying up there, about a thousand feet above us. We daren't pull our noses up to try and make up that thousand feet, because it would have reduced our speed too much and made us far too easy a target. We were climbing at our maximum rate at that altitude, maybe a hundred feet a minute – certainly not more. With luck we might be up on their level by the time we got somewhere near France, but the chances were that they'd start increasing height themselves.

Suddenly, two of the Huns dived and took a quick spray at us, climbing back out of reach before we could do anything about it. So that was the game, was it? Quickly we split, each flight going on either side of them, and we just waited for the next pair to come down. Sure enough they did, and as they did so a pair from the other flight in my squadron turned across in an effort to catch them before they could climb up again, but it wasn't any good – they were wily, as well as yellow. We'd almost reached the French coast by now and had had quite a long chase, preceded by a fast climb. We couldn't afford to hang around as there was no telling if there might be another formation of Huns coming up to chase us back; in which case we'd need every ounce of petrol we had, so we turned round and made for home without having fired a shot.

After landing, when the aircraft were refuelled and the squadron was back at immediate readiness, I shambled over to the telephone and had a few words with Ops. Apparently, there was absolutely nothing doing – not even a reconnaissance aircraft about. I went out into the sun. Might as well get sunburnt. Somehow, one always felt better when one looked in the mirror in the morning and saw a decently sunburnt face. The green pallor left after the party of the night before didn't show up so much, and although you might feel like death, you certainly didn't look it, which is always some sort of a consolation. I lay down in the long grass, using an aircraft chock as a headrest, closed my eyes and let my mind wander. Then suddenly I was brought to my senses by a yell: Scramble! Everybody was dashing about, the usual scene was taking place just before take-off. I felt drowsy and very much disinclined to go and chase the Hun or be chased by him. However, off we went; as usual we clambered up to 30,000 ft and on the way up I couldn't help thinking about the lunch that we were leaving behind, because I noticed that it was now almost lunch-time. We wheeled away to the south-east. Apparently the break we'd had this morning was indeed the lull before the storm, for the Hun seemed to be sending in sweep after sweep across the coast – most probably only fighters, but you never can tell: there might be the odd bomber formations slipped in between. We hadn't been at 30,000 ft for more than a minute when we saw the first Huns. Were we in luck? The formation was about 2,000 ft below and dead ahead. Then we saw another formation above and up-sun! Those wily devils had laid a trap but we hadn't fallen for it. Instead we wheeled into the sun and went straight for the high cover. They were only a matter of a 1,000 ft above us and our move was so unexpected that we rather caught them napping. They broke up as we got to them, and dived like the frightened bunch of rats they were. One of them most certainly never pulled out. I couldn't follow him, but he was on fire as he went and we were still in pretty good formation.

We turned and chased the other bunch that had been below us. They had shoved off for France in a hurry thinking that their friends up-sun had taken care of us. They literally didn't see us and had no idea that we'd started our attack until three of them went down in flames. But we no sooner started the attack than we ourselves were jumped. Another wave had arrived overhead at least 3,000 ft above us and they came hurtling down at us straight out of the sun. Buster Squadron rallied beautifully in spite of the fact that we'd been jumped. Half of our pilots climbed to face the diving Huns (there's nothing like putting on a bold face when you're in a tight corner). This time, however, it was too late for the *jagdgeschwader* to turn tail: they simply couldn't stop their attack and they were met by four Spitfires coming straight up at them with guns firing. I couldn't see what happened to them after that; in fact I'd been lucky to be able to watch that much of the combat, for I was just closing in on another Hun and was getting all set to give him a burst, when I felt a judder as some German bullets hit my Spitfire. Next moment a cannon shell burst on the starboard wing root, and at the same instant there was a damned unpleasant pain in my leg. As all this was happening I'd been pressing the firing button and by some strange coincidence the Hun in front of me broke in the same direction as I broke when I was hit. I followed him around and got in another quick burst, which sent him down out of control. The other little bastard was still on my tail, however, and I had to shake him off before I could do anything more. My leg was beginning to hurt quite a lot. I hauled the gee even more and could see him vainly struggling to follow me round, but it wasn't any good; I was turning quite easily inside him. If he'd stick, I'd be able to get on to his tail, but just as I thought he was going to be sucker enough to stay put, another Spitfire came to my assistance. The Hun must have been so engrossed in trying to catch me up that he couldn't have seen the other bloke coming. It must have been a direct hit in the petrol tank, because he exploded into tiny pieces.

I straightened out for an instant to watch him go down, then as I looked round again for something to shoot at, I saw a Spitfire hurtling down at me. Was the fellow going to take a pot-shot at me? I yelled at him over the R/T but he came straight on down. I turned in underneath him, but he tried to follow. I cursed the pilot for being a bloody fool, but it's all very difficult in the heat of battle. My trousers had by now begun to stick to my leg and I found that I couldn't put the full pressure of my left foot on the rudder bar. I wound the rudder bias to ease the situation. I still had some ammunition, and I thought I might be able to make good if only I could tag on to another Hun in time.

The sky was a whirling mass of machines. I could see four parachutes drifting down slowly below me and there was an aircraft streaking down over to my starboard in flames – the pilot dangling on his parachute about 3,000 ft above. Just at that moment I caught sight of another Spitfire. He'd got a couple of Messerschmitts on his tail. By luck I happened to be up-sun of them, so I turned and sprayed them with my eight Brownings, but not quite in time, I'm afraid. There was an explosion and the Spitfire came to bits. It must have been a direct hit in the petrol tanks. As I sprayed them, still at fairly long range, the rearmost one in line broke away and went into a vertical dive. I think he was just getting out of the way, but the leader must have been too interested in watching the Spitfire falling in flames, for he started circling. Now was my chance! I got up close to him and slightly underneath him – then I pulled the stick back, pressed the tit. There was an explosion and he burst into a sheet of flame from the cockpit to the tail. The machine levelled out and the pilot started to climb out. I gave another short burst; the pilot seemed to straighten up in the cockpit and then sagged over the side. That was one Hun less.

In the meantime, I'd made that unforgivable mistake of not watching my own tail. My Spitfire shuddered and there was an explosion, the cockpit canopy disintegrated and my instruments began to fall apart. Petrol began gushing into the cockpit. I stamped my right foot down on the rudder and pulled the stick back hard and then reversed the process and streaked down towards the ground. The petrol was getting in my eyes, I couldn't see a damn thing. Thank God it hadn't caught fire. I was soaked to the skin and my neck was hurting like hell. I expect I'd been wounded again, but by now all I was concerned with was getting out of that Spitfire just as quickly as I could. There were only two instruments on the panel that were working. I suddenly appreciated that my right arm didn't seem to be there, and although I exerted all my strength of will, I couldn't make my hand pull the stick back. I realized that in spite of the ice-cold of the petrol, the back of my arm felt hot and sticky. I whipped my goggles off and tried rubbing the petrol out of my eyes, but that only made it worse. I pushed them back again and getting my left hand on the stick I began to pull out of the dive. I'd no idea what height I was at, for I'd been going down for what seemed an age. I must be bloody close to the deck.

My neck and leg were stinging like hell as the petrol penetrated into the wounds and I felt strangely faint. I whipped my oxygen mask off and the next moment got a mouthful of petrol. That was no good. I couldn't possibly put the mask back, and yet every time I breathed I stood a good chance of getting another mouthful. I heaved at the lever and thank God the canopy opened; I pushed my face out over the side and hoped for the best. I began to think a bit more clearly now and realized how lucky I was that the machine was not on fire. If it had caught fire and even if I then baled-out, I would have been burnt to a cinder, my clothes and parachute being by now absolutely saturated in petrol. I still felt faint and a strong feeling of nausea began to creep over me. The question was, could I land this sieve of mine or would it be better to bale-out? I hadn't the vaguest idea where I was now, I'd been going round in circles for about five minutes trying to clear my head and reach some rational decision. I felt for my map, but couldn't find it. I'd have to do something damn quick, there was always the chance that the Spitfire might catch fire and explode at any moment. In any case, I realized when I calculated my chances of being able to get back to base before the petrol ran out that I was obviously going to run dry of fuel. Of course it would be ideal to get the machine back almost in one piece, but at the rate the petrol was pouring into the cockpit, I thought it better not to take the chance. If the engine did conk out half-way there, the possibility of getting her down in a field in one piece would be very much against me.

I stuck my head further out into the clean air, the tears caused by the petrol soon began to clear and I was again able to see the ground more or less clearly. There were quite a number of possible fields where I could belly-land, but damn me if they were not all barricaded against the invasion. Here was a pretty pickle! What the hell was I going to do now? I flew around for a couple of minutes looking at one very big field and decided that, with luck, I could land in between all the obstructions. I made a careful note of the line of approach, selected undercarriage down, and then the flaps; I was determined to get the machine on the ground in as much of one piece as possible. Then I started throttling back with a nasty feeling that sparks, which usually occur as one throttles back, might set the machine alight. If they did, there wasn't a hope in hell. A pity if it ended like that, having got away with so much already. The only thing to do was to cut the magneto switches and hope to God that my judgment of the height was good enough. I held my breath, I was over-shooting; a quick side slip and we landed with a hell of a thud! I jammed on the brakes and worked frantically to keep her straight. Poles were whizzing by on either side: a wrecked car acting as a barricade loomed up, but my wing-tip just cleared it. Gradually we slowed. Then I was brought up with a tremendous jerk – I had gone head-on into another wrecked car, but fortunately it did nothing more than snap one of the blades off the propeller! I remained seated in the cockpit for a few moments, not quite sure what to do; I just didn't know. Then the pain in my neck, arm and leg roused me into action; I felt absolutely frozen in my bath of petrol, so I started climbing out. My right arm had gradually come back to life and was hurting quite a bit.

As I clambered out of the cockpit, half hopping and half sliding, and got to the ground, the Home Guard, and I should think the whole population of the local village arrived on the scene. There were too many people smoking. Petrol was still pouring out of the machine and they wanted to clamber all over it with lighted cigarettes and pipes. However, they were very good about it all and the local policeman and two of the Home Guard soon made everyone keep a safe distance from the aircraft. The trouble was, I wanted a smoke myself, but I daren't have one because my flying overall was still saturated with petrol. I found I could walk all right, but my neck felt pretty stiff and my arm was still useless. Leaving the local copper and Home Guard in charge, I was whisked away by a local ambulance party to a neighbouring First-Aid Centre. I must say I felt the need of a little attention right then. What I wanted most was a cup of very hot and very sweet tea, and I felt sure that, rationing or not, I was going to get it this time.

They patched up my wounds and got hold of an RAF car from the nearest station. I was driven back to my base to the sick quarters. The medical officer took one look at me and said sorry old boy, we'll have to take some of this lead out. So with another cup of hot tea, this time with all the sugar I wanted, plus a liberal ration of rum I stretched out and the brute got down to work. I can't tell you how much more painful it was having the lead taken out than pushed in!

After a long time of juggling about with probes and forceps they got all the big chunks of lead out. I reckoned that was enough for one day, and as they put the dressing on, was planning what sort of party I'd be having that night. Then the doctor said I'd have to get to bed! That was too much. Normally, I'm very amenable to discipline, but hell, not after today. Strong drink was indicated. It took me a long time to persuade the doc that putting me to bed would be absolutely futile but then he let me roam off to the mess for a meal. After my lunch-cum-tea, I ambled down to the dispersal. Nobody had seen poor old Jim go, but they found his machine and it had dug itself in deep. There were three others wounded besides myself on that sortie, but fortunately, only one seriously and it looked as if he would have to lose his right leg: a bloody shame. On the other hand, better that than pushing up daisies.

*　　*　　*

RUFUS was older than average and had been around a bit, quite a bit. He had been educated at a public school; so had quite a number of the other pilots on Buster Squadron. Not that we wore old school ties; when we did wear a tie it was RAF uniform black, appropriate to the state of mourning we usually found ourselves in. Rufus looked in profile like the devil; strong nose, uplifted eyebrows, cruel mouth, deep-set eyes. In countenance he looked like the charming man he was, green eyes, crooked mouth, slightly misshappen teeth, a pleasant grin, beautifully trimmed hair, strong hands and well-manicured finger nails. Rufus was God's gift to women and he knew it; nevertheless he was selective. Rufus wasn't like Randy; he didn't consort with shop-girls; he preferred countesses, young countesses, or innocent debutantes.

I suspect, in fact, that Rufus was the nicest chap I ever met in my life. I don't believe that Casanova was particularly nice but Rufus could be compared with him in certain ways. His wine bill in the mess, if you can call the shack we lived in a mess, was phenomenal. His idea of a lark was to take-off and fly as near Berlin as possible, shooting down Huns en route. He broke cars with monotonous regularity in head-on collisions, mainly because he was tight as a drum. He always managed to turn out looking dapper, even in the field conditions we lived under. His suits and uniforms were created by the best tailor in London, his shoes were made by Lobb and he had a standing arrangement with a London barber who would drive out to the airfield and trim his hair weekly. He was a Judo expert, tough as an ox and he spoke fluent French. He could have made a fortune as an actor, as a professional gigolo, or as a con-man. I adored Rufus.

The manner of his death was unbecoming. He was a positive wizard as a fighter pilot and wore the DFC and bar. One day he was outnumbered by six Messerschmitts who blew him into thin air just beyond Dover harbour; he was, naturally, flying a Spitfire. Only a race-horse would have done for him. That old hack, the Hurricane, would have bored him out of his mind.

He had been a very great artist in all senses of the word. His technique had been so cerebral, his knowledge so complex. Like Vermeer in artistic terms, Rufus was a genius.

'Blow out, you bugles, over the rich dead.'

CHAPTER TEN

BUTCH

My Merlin engine wouldn't start, which sometimes occurs, and the squadron took-off to sweep Dunkirk minus me. The Flight Sergeant Engine Fitter ran across and I suggested the battery might be somewhat run down. He hastily ordered a team of men to wheel another one over while he disengaged the big plug from my Spitfire. The airmen positively sprinted, hauling the large starter battery on its rubber wheels behind them like a minor stage-coach being pulled by four horses. The Flight Sergeant plugged it in and the men heaved the other one out of harm's way.

'The plugs might be wet now,' the Flight Sergeant warned me.

'O.K. But it's worth a try,' I replied.

I pressed the starting tit, the three-bladed propeller turned and gathered momentum and then the Merlin fired. The black smoke issuing from the exhausts indicated that the plugs were wet, but the engine was warm enough for take off, so I pulled the control column back to keep the tail down and gave her a bit of boost to clean the plugs. The Spitfire is very sensitive fore and aft and indeed in a strong wind one has to have two airmen sitting on the tail to ensure she isn't blown on her nose. I once started to take-off with two men on my tail, but fortunately remembered they were there when the speed increased to about 20 mph. They were nearly blown off at that stage though and I told them I was extremely sorry for my lapse.

I waved the chocks away, taxied to the take-off point of the grass airfield, noted that the wind sock indicated a wind speed of about 15 mph, opened the throttle and she roared into the air. I retracted my under-cart at about ten feet and closed the radiator shutter. The radiator has to be open for taxiing and take-off, but the flow of air when in flight keeps the Merlin cool enough; in any case, with the shutter in the down position it would cause drag to the detriment of her performance flat out. She gathered speed and I kept her down to around fifty feet because my intention was to fly to Dunkirk at low level. The squadron commander's brief had been to act as top cover flying at 27,000 ft which was bloody silly. We were supposed to be there to protect the BEF not fart around looking for mythical Messerschmitts, so top and medium cover was not only totally irrelevant, it also meant that we would be in no position to get among the German bombers. Someone in Fighter Command Headquarters needed his head examined by a very senior phrenologist.

I put the mixture on to weak to conserve fuel, throttled back when she gained speed to 250 mph for the same reason, put the oxygen on to emergency to make sure the system was working, and the ice cold flow on my palate told me that it was. I then turned it off because I didn't need any oxygen at 50 ft. I turned on to a course of about due east which allowing for wind drift should get me to Dunkirk and then checked the compass with the sun's position. The coast of Suffolk drifted past my wing and then I was over the cold North Sea. Before long I didn't need to maintain course through my gyro-compass because there was a veritable armada of ships, both big and small, sailing to England from Dunkirk and others were returning to pick up more British and French troops. So I just flew over them in the direction those returning to France were going.

It took me almost half an hour to reach Dunkirk and as I approached I saw a great cloud of black smoke which must have meant that an oil refinery had been set on fire. When I was about ten miles from the port, I gave the Spitfire full boost and climbed as fast as I could without losing reasonable combat speed. I gazed down and saw horrible things like columns of troops on the beaches and even off shore. Little boats, paddle steamers, destroyers and so on were there getting men aboard. I was now at about 10,000 ft, a nice combat altitude, which was where Buster Squadron should have been, not farting around above the cirrus. A gaggle of Junkers 87 materialized above me and went into a near vertical dive to bomb the beaches. I should have climbed higher because the Stukas tend to start their dive-bombing attacks at around 15,000 ft. Having made this error of judgment I could do nothing to stop their bombs being aimed, because they were near vertical on the dive and had dive brakes; I would have overshot them if I had tried to go down at an angle of 80 degrees.

The only option open to me was to throttle right back and spiral down in a gliding turn. I kept them – there were six I think – in sight but could not get in range to fire at them. However, when I saw their bombs fly down, when I saw them haul out of the dive, they were suckers. They each had only one rear gun and could hardly exceed 150 mph straight and level. I latched on to the leader of the formation and his gunner shot a hail of tracer at me. I skidded to port and came in on a quarter attack which was well outside his arc of fire. At about 350 yards I lined him up in my gunsight at an angle of about 30 degrees and then pressed the firing tit. He exploded quicker than a whore can get her knickers down in front of a millionaire. When I jacked the Spitfire round there was another approaching me almost head on. We were at about fifty feet at this time and the Ju 87 wobbled as the pilot saw me coming in on a head-on attack. He dived a bit and hit a tree. Finis!

I could see no more German – or British – aircraft and had used up quite a lot of fuel by using emergency boost on the climb. There was a mist over the sea and I worked it out that I had better run for home in case I got lost. My gyro-compass had spun during combat and I didn't trust the magnetic compass too much as it was swinging like a dancer doing the tango. Nor could I see the sun any longer, so I set course using as my navigational aids the ships that were sailing back to England. I arrived back somewhere over the Thames estuary but I thought I was over Antwerp. I flew low until I noted that the traffic was being driven on the left-hand side of the roads and thereby established the fact that I was indeed over England. I managed to get back to my home base by following railway lines and reading the names of the stations. I landed with twenty gallons of petrol in the tanks and I had used up only about 300 rounds on the Hun I shot down.

*   *   *

It's a funny business being a fighter pilot. Of an evening you can be at the cinema with your girl friend putting your hand up her skirt unless, that is to say, you are on full moon night standby. But well before first light you may be at operational readiness, you may be engaging the enemy all day long, and when dusk falls you are probably too tired to cope with your girl friend. I am young and fit, but my God, flying five or more sorties a day at altitudes of over 30,000 ft makes you bone weary. We dare not eat peas because the rarified atmosphere would cause you to fart your head off. In fact we are light eaters. In any case, half-way through a meal more likely than not, the scramble order would be given. And what a waste of food that represented. Things hotted up like hell when we were deployed to 11 Group when the Battle of Britain began to warn up somewhat. I flew the first sortie in my pyjamas almost every day, and I hardly had time to shave ahead of the scramble order.

But those possible or probable last moments of living on earth made one realize that life is, after all, worthwhile. The smell of the grass was a thing one had never really appreciated before. The red buses might cause traffic jams, but they are somehow a symbol of living. People are the most important aspect of life, but you don't appreciate that until you are sent off on what might be your final flight. Of course there was a tremendous camaradarie in Buster Squadron, between officer and sergeant pilots and ground crews. We were a very tightly knit team; it was like being in church in a strange sort of manner. We didn't have church music but my God we did have our pornographic ballads, which we sang with our tankards of beer clasped firmly in our hands. We were just like a lot of choir boys in certain respects. Part of a parson's job is to christen babies and fulfil the funeral rites. We did this too. We had to attempt to train new trainee pilots when they arrived on the squadron not knowing their arses from their elbows; and we had to bury those who were killed in action. The casualty rate was appalling. I could see a chap due to buy his purchase to heaven almost at a glance. For all I know, some of my fellow pilots can see the look of death on my face – I don't know about that. Rupert Brooke who was killed in 1915 obviously had the same experience of the last moments of living that I have. As he was in danger of death he appreciated the little things of life all the more. It is really remarkable that I should sense things – like the smell of grass – which had meant nothing to me before.

Not a bad example of what I mean: Brooke wrote 'Live hair that is shining and free; blue-massing clouds; the keen unpassioned beauty of a great machine; the benison of hot water; furs to touch; the good smell of old clothes.' That is almost exactly how I feel when the scramble order arrives over the field telephone. I mean, how stupid we are to ignore or neglect these strange but all-important aspects of living.

Anyhow, at the most ferocious period during the Battle of Britain, I was stupid enough to engage the *jagdgeschwader* of the Luftwaffe single-handed. I was stupid because there were fifty Messerschmitts in the formation and I was on my own carrying out an air test on a Spitfire Mk II. I was even more stupid than that because my Spitfire was not fully serviceable, which fact I diagnosed during the air test. However, the guns were, as usual, fully loaded so when I heard on the R/T frequency the fighter controller reporting a plot indicating fifty plus bandits crossing the coast somewhere near Dungeness, I climbed to see if I could engage any Huns. The cloud formed a layer, base 15,000 ft, top 20,000 ft and I had no oxygen because the system was unserviceable. This might have accounted for my further stupidity; in other words my brain must have been fuzzed, as anoxia normally starts to set in at about 15,000 ft.

The moment I broke cloud, if it is appreciated that the Messerschmitts were 10,000 ft above me, up-sun and with plenty of fuel, it must be obvious that my Spitfire would have been clearly silhouetted against the layer of cloud, easily recognizable to the eyes of fifty German fighter pilots nicely positioned above.

'*Achtung* Spitfire!' must have been the cry of delight over the Germans' R/T, and if so, the *jagdgeschwader* leader would have detached half a dozen Me 109s to knock me off. By this time, the Messerschmitt 109 was fitted with two 20 mm cannon as well as machine-guns. The Spitfire still retained the inadequate battery of eight light machine-guns. The fluid tactics of the fighter arm of the Luftwaffe were reliant upon a basic formation of four aircraft easily deployable into sections of twos; this was the essential fighting formation which Fighter Command did not operate. More likely than not, therefore, the leader of the Messerschmitt formation dispatched eight, not six, Me 109s into a vertical dive to deal with my Spitfire.

I saw them coming, hauled back on the control column and manoeuvred the Spitfire in a vertical climb facing the onslaught. As the first four Messerschmitts came down at very high speed into my gunsight, I pressed the firing-button when the aircraft of the Luftwaffe were, in theory, out of range. Due to the fast closing speed, however, the Messerschmitts, so to speak, ran headlong into my bullets. The wing of one Me 109 was struck with such force that it tore off, the fuselage of the aircraft careered sideways and hit its number two. The two Messerschmitts locked themselves together, fluttered and dropped into the sea just off Sandwich. Ground observers took note of the disposition of the grave of two German pilots.

I stalled off the climb, not unnaturally, and fell helpless as a pinioned duck. The probable six German pilots who were still breathing put all their nerve into killing me, because I had killed two of their colleagues. They had the advantage of numbers and tactical conditions, also very much heavier armament. One German pilot gave me a blast from about 200 yards. This resulted in my Spitfire receiving 43 holes from machine-guns and a big chunk out of it from an explosive cannon-shell, as my ground crew discovered later. The armour-plate protecting my back was pierced and bits of lead together with steel splinters from the armour plate penetrated my right arm, my master arm. One bullet hurtled through my right bicep and the shock wave severely bruised the ribs on the right side of my body. My gauntleted hand was willy-nilly thrown up with great force by the shock wave, my hand struck the cockpit canopy which splintered, and the knuckles were thus very severely bruised.

My right arm was now hanging limply down, useless, so I transferred my left hand to the control column of the Spitfire. I did not open the throttle wide at this stage because I wanted to turn inside the Messerschmitt which had assailed me. The more engine power, the wider the turning circle of the fighter, granted equal gee forces. In this manner I turned inside the Messerschmitt, then I had to transfer my left hand to the throttle lever thus momentarily losing control of the Spitfire. I thrust the throttle wide and broke the seals on the quadrant in order to attain emergency boost, whereupon black smoke poured from the exhaust stubs of my Spitfire, which might have caused the German pilots all massing for the kill to believe that my aircraft had begun to burn. I hauled the Spitfire round at four plus gee and closed range to 200 yards behind the Me 109 which had bust my right arm.

I pressed the firing button and the Messerschmitt 109 blew up in my face. Chunks of debris clattered against my fuselage and I instinctively ducked. I got out of it by diving into the God-sent invisibility of the clouds. I then transferred my left hand from the control column to the throttle, pulled it right back to tick-over point, allowed a little time for the airspeed to cool down from 500 mph to about 200 mph, rolled the Spitfire into an inverted position and heaved back on the stick. This put the aircraft into a vertical dive; I was still in cloud.

I continued this dive, speed quickly increasing despite the lack of engine power, and I hauled it out of the dive at 1,500 ft. The forces took the aircraft down to 200 ft above ground level before she was flying straight and level. Whereupon I transferred my left hand from the control column to the throttle, adjusted for cruising revs, and flew left-handed back to my base at tree-top height. My R/T was not working because the radio had exploded under the impact of German fire; the flaps were unserviceable and the electric systems were bust wide open. Further to which, although I did not realize it at the time, some of my control cables were hanging on by mere threads.

My Spitfire was inspected when I managed to land without further harm. I was taken to hospital and operated on; my Spitfire was not so fortunate. She was simply placed Category Four – written off as a wreck from which nothing was worth salvaging. My Spitfire wasn't driven to hospital, it was just chucked on the scrap-heap.

*   *   *

BUTCH was another of the exceptional fighter pilots in Buster Squadron who merited the award of the Victoria Cross among other things. Butch was short, stocky and red-haired with a lazy grin, which was about the only lazy thing in his make-up. There can be little doubt that he had been a kind of cat in a previous incarnation, probably a leopard if not a tiger. His reflexes were so sharp that he almost seemed to know what you were doing before you did it. He was so long-sighted that he could almost see the great wall of China when standing on the Malvern Heights. Long-sightedness is most important in fighter combat but Butch improved even on that. He was intelligent enough to realize that even the best of eyesight has to work without a frame of reference when peering into thin air at great height. Although in theory anyone looking at the stars, for example, focuses on infinity, some people, and Butch was one of them, can train themselves to see beyond infinity, as it were.

Butch also used to take a greater than average interest in his Spitfire, especially the guns and gun-sight. The eight Brownings in the Spitfire were disposed quite widely apart from each other in the wings, and the gun sight itself in the pilot's cockpit was several feet above the guns. Thus there came the need for harmonization, as we termed the process. If Butch suffered from nerves consequent on battle strain, he did not show it. Most pilots managed to conceal this aspect but to a discerning judge some gave away their innermost feelings. It was not surprising that nerves did get stretched; on many days we flew six sorties a day on operations and possibly another on our air tests to ensure our Spitfires were serviceable. On about forty per cent of our scrambles we saw nothing and were not engaged, but that didn't mean to say that the nervous tension was not there, because we never knew whether we were going to be bounced by Luftwaffe fighters or not. And they bounced us on a far greater number of occasions than we did them, because they normally had the advantage of height, of speed as we were often on the climb when they arrived, and of weight of armament.

Butch flew on every sortie for which he was detailed, which does not imply that he flew on every individual squadron sortie. There had to be some sort of roster system, partly to give newly-joined pilots a chance of gaining combat experience; partly to give experienced pilots the chance of a rest. In the same manner, as far as possible, squadrons were rotated as to states of readiness — immediate, fifteen minutes, thirty minutes or even released. The system didn't work of course; Buster Squadron was scrambled from a released posture on many occasions. The pilots who really took the brunt of almost non-stop operations were the squadron and flight commanders, also some section leaders. The total leadership of the British fighter force in 1940 was in the hands of less than 500 men; the fact that approximately 3,500 pilots and aircrew were given the Battle of Britain medal clasp is grossly misleading.

However, Butch died as I thought he would die, in a kind of Victoria Cross action. The last I saw of Butch's Spitfire was when its airscrew was cutting off the tail-fin of a Messerschmitt 109. I can't prove it, but I have little doubt that he had run out of ammunition, or his guns wouldn't work, and he decided on ramming tactics. He must have been intending to bale out when he had destroyed the Me 109 and, pari passu, his own Spitfire, but he didn't have a chance. The two fighters locked themselves together in deadly embrace and fell like the autumn foliage, only with considerably greater speed, and descended vertically from 25,000 ft, straight into the English Channel.

Dryden must have foreseen it: 'When rattling bones together fly from the four corners of the sky.'

EPITAPH

'Me miserable! which way shall I fly
Infinite wrath, and infinite despair?
Which way I fly is hell; myself am hell;
And in the lowest deep a lower deep
Still threatening to devour me opens wide,
To which the hell I suffer seems a heaven.'*

* John Milton.

THEY CAME FROM THE SKY BY E. H. COOKRIDGE

The Special Operations Executive was created by Churchill in the Summer of 1940 to 'set Europe ablaze'. Working secretly behind enemy lines to 'sabotage and subvert', they operated all over Europe, and some of the most active agents were in the French Section. It was dangerous work, and many agents did not return: a few, like Christine Granville, became famous names, but for the most part their exploits remain unsung. Here now are the stories of three members of the French Section – true stories that make more exciting reading than any novel . . . They had little training, and their unconventional methods were frowned on by the top brass of the Army, but what they lacked in style, they more than made up for in courage and initiative . . .

0 552 10136 2   75p

THE SAVAGE CANARY BY DAVID LAMPE

The Danish resistance movement was described by Montgomery as 'second to none'.

The Savage Canary is a fantastic but true account of the Danish efforts to help the Allies and cripple Germany in the Second World War. By May 1945, illegal newspapers had published a total of about 26 million issues; illegal broadcasts were transmitted regularly; boats were running a timetable service between Britain, Sweden and Denmark and 7,000 Jews had been shipped to safety. German ships were unable to move from Danish harbours; a vast number of German troops were kept from the main fighting points by Danish sabotage of the railways and aerodromes. This book, the story of an impudent, almost foolhardy heroism, is a salute to the people of Denmark.

0 552 10101 X   65p

A SELECTED LIST OF WAR BOOKS PUBLISHED BY CORGI

All these books are available at your bookshop or newsagent, or can be ordered direct from the publisher. Just tick the titles you want and fill in the form below.

CORGI BOOKS, Cash Sales Department, P.O. Box 11, Falmouth, Cornwall.

Please send cheque or postal order, no currency.
U.K. send 19p for first book plus 9p per copy for each additional book ordered to a maximum charge of 73p to cover the cost of postage and packing.
B.F.P.O. and Eire allow 19p for first book plus 9p per copy for the next 6 books thereafter 3p per book.
Overseas Customers: Please allow 20p for the first book and 10p per copy for each additional book.

NAME (Block letters) ....

ADDRESS ....

(DEC. 76) ....